Between the Lines...
Beyond the Pain

Dawn Forman

may the one who reads
this book find healing
in its pages.
♡

Between the Lines...
Beyond the Pain

D A W N   F O R M A N

Between the Lines . . . Beyond the Pain

Published by Wheatmark®
2030 East Speedway Boulevard, Suite 106
Tucson, Arizona 85719 USA
www.wheatmark.com

ISBN: 978-1-62787-543-1
LCCN: 2017947413

Contents

Stars   3

Behind the Sorrow Lines   6

Behind the Laugh Lines   13

Behind the Boundary Lines   20

Between the Lines   31

Blurred Lines   42

Beyond the Pain   128

Dedicated to all who have ever been heartbroken.

*Special thanks to Kari Czer for making the
publication of this book possible.*

Stars

THE STARS CANNOT BE seen until they are set against the ebony background of the night sky. They are always there, but they remain invisible to us, unnoticeable, unappreciated, unvalued, until the contrast of the darkness behind them brings to our attention their shining beauty. So it is with many of the people with whom we share the planet. Some of them nameless faces we pass in our daily routines, others are part of our inner circle in one way or another, but they are beings that we overlook because we find them to be either difficult, abrasive, pathetic or just nondescript. Should we somehow discover the dark background of their past, their struggles and sufferings, for there is always a story behind the story; people are the way they are for a reason, they too, in contrast, would shine as stars or heroes to us for what they have endured or overcome in their lives. Like the stars in the night sky, they would suddenly be seen and appreciated. Their words would take on new meaning, falling on ears that would hear them filtered through a heart of compassion as we learn to see and read and live between the lines.

How different life looks through the mist of sadness. Some things are too painful to be spoken. Stuffed down and guarded in our heart they seem to be muffled, as if shrouded in cotton, lying dormant only half true and half alive. To speak them aloud and give them life would be like removing an antique bottle from its padded box and letting it fall to the ground, shattering into too many fragments to ever be put back together. So it would be with our heart if we spoke the pains and wounds bottled up inside of us. Better to keep them in the padded walls of silence than to let the shrill of their reality be spoken, shattering us forever... or is it? Keeping the bottle tightly sealed and guarded, its contents can turn into poison. What if breaking the bottle open meant that its contents would be a healing balm for someone else? It might be not only a healing for someone else but cathartic for us at the same time. What if what we choose to do with our pain either makes us or breaks us? Everyone bleeds when they are cut, everyone sheds tears when they are hurt, yet everyone responds differently to the deep disappointments and sorrows in life. We all have the same options, but we do not all make the same choices about where to go or how to proceed once we pick ourselves back up after being knocked or dragged down by the sufferings that sometimes blindside us. Will we remain broken, or be determined to find beauty in our brokenness? What will we do with the fragmented pieces of our life? Guard them in a shrine? Throw them in the trash? Or,...ever see a beautiful mosaic piece of art that brings joy and awe to all who observe it? We do not have the privilege of choosing whether or not we will experience pain in this life. It comes to us all. The only choice we do have is what we will do with that pain. The people in the following stories are but a few examples of human nature when confronted with agonizing situations. I imagine since people are so diverse, the possibilities of their reactions to pain and suffering are as limitless as... the stars in the sky.

Behind the Sorrow Lines

IT WAS A TUESDAY. I love Tuesdays. They are packed full from the time I stumble out of bed until the time I crawl back in at night exhausted, but I love them. I teach elementary school Monday through Friday, and after school on Tuesdays I morph from teacher to student as I sit among a melting pot of other older adults in my French Literature class. That's the title of the course anyway, French Literature, but it is actually more of a book club. We read novels in French and then discuss the style of writing, author, storyline plots and characters. Some people have been coming for over 10 years. I call it a melting pot because there are people representing about 15 different countries in this class. Some of them are more colorful characters than those in the novels we read. Though they are of a certain age that some call elderly, they are interesting, intelligent, cultured, wealthy or poor, but most of all lovers of literature and French. In between the books we read, and the few lines spoken to one another in class, lies a bountiful harvest of beautiful souls, invisible stars struggling to shine in this dark world. Among them is Meesha. Meesha is 75, tall, and has hair that is two toned. It is white and reddish brown, due to the fact she has recently decided to stop coloring her hair. She is always wearing something handmade, made by her own hands. She can make just about anything from knitted scarves to jewelry, dresses, purses, and even the best homemade French Macarons I have ever tasted. She was a nurse before she retired, she is also an atheist. At first meeting, she might seem gruff, cold, and distant. A tough bird one might say. She says what she thinks with no shame, which might be interpreted as no concern for others, but it is not true. Underneath the tough exterior beats a tender, though battered heart. I have come to know and love her.

One day, before class started, there was a group of us involved in a discussion as to why people these days use the expression, "I need to find myself." My comment was that I believe what people mean by that really is that they want to find some meaning to their life before they die. Meesha's addition to the conversation was, " I don't need to find myself; I know exactly who I am, I am Meesha, born of Italian parents in Israel, and when you're dead you're dead! There IS NO MEANING!" As I said, she can come across as gruff, even callous to those who don't know her. It might seem that all her comments are negative, cynical and angry. Yet, knowing her story changes everything. For me that day, as she declared those words it was like a bell going off in my head. Her words triggered in my mind the series of events in her life that would cause her to say what she did, and I had nothing but compassion for this wounded soul. What rose up and screamed inside of me was a voice saying, "Read between the lines!" Between the lines of the phrase she uttered, behind the lines of her weathered face, there is a story. After all, one is not born an atheist OR a believer in God; conclusions are drawn from our experiences in life.

Hearing Meesha's harsh words, one might think, "Ah, I know exactly what kind of nurse she was! The kind who takes pleasure in giving you shots and placing catheters, and smiles at your pain!" But that is not the truth. The truth lies behind the sorrow etched lines on her face.

Trained as a young nurse in Israel, she was required to do her internship in several areas in the hospital before being able to choose which department she wanted to stay and work in. One of those areas was Pediatrics. I asked her once what was the most difficult experience she ever faced as a nurse. She said, "I remember it like it was yesterday"; this is the story she recounted to me.

There was a young boy, maybe 7 or 8 years of age, who had bone cancer. Day by day, the cruelty of the disease became more visible. She could see his jawbone being eaten away. Each night she could hear him scream out in pain. The treatments were no longer working. Nothing could be done as she was forced to helplessly watch this poor child's life ebb away. As she returned home each night after her shift she could not shake it off and forget but was so haunted by his screams and the vision of his young, sweet, yet deteriorating face, that she could no longer eat or sleep.

Taking its toll not only mentally and emotionally but also physically to the point that she lost 20 pounds in 3 weeks! She begged to never return to the Pediatrics department.

Not long after, Meesha fell in love. They were married, life was bright and her future hopeful. Soon to follow was her burgeoning belly and a shared joy as they discussed plans for their developing family. Then came the news that her beloved husband was being called to fulfill his obligatory service in the army. One minute their hearts were bursting with the joy of their upcoming child, the next their hearts beat as one in fear as they lingered in a long and tearful embrace. It was the last one they ever shared; her husband was killed in the war. They had only been married 6 months. Her son was born and never knew his father. She never remarried. She never fully recovered.

A young child dying a slow, cruel, painful death? A beloved husband senselessly taken too soon? How could she possibly believe there is a God? How could she believe that there is any meaning to life? Though most would judge her and bristle at her harsh words, "When you're dead you're dead, there IS NO meaning," I was moved by compassion because I know her story. I could easily trace the path she must have walked that led her to where and what she is today. I could see the burden upon her shoulders that weighed her down, down, down to the point of drawing this hopeless conclusion that there is no meaning to life. I could feel in my own heart the gut wrenching tears of sorrow she must have cried. I wish I could tell you more about her life, but she says very little. I know she has a brother she has not spoken to in 40 years. I know that she says her childhood was a markedly painful one. She will not give details. She does not like to talk about herself and chooses to remain bottled up. A tough old bird bottled up full of cynicism, wherein the hero? She did not allow her pain to cause her to hide or recoil into a cave. On the contrary, she has been an extremely productive person. She is 75, and though retired, she takes several classes everyday at the senior's college, and as I mentioned before, she uses her time to make just about anything. She is intelligent and productive, yet, her pain remains. Though she did not slay the dragon of sorrow, neither did she let the dragon slay her. Although, one must concede that she remains somewhat singed by its fiery breath. The burden she has borne so many years is evident by her weighted down shoulders and bowed head.

I decided to just be loving to her no matter what. I know she loves ladybugs so one day when I was in a market and saw pieces of chocolate wrapped in foil to look like ladybugs I bought her one and brought it to class. I gave her a ride home once when it was raining. I overheard one day that the following class would be her birthday so I brought a card and a small gift. Another day, she had missed a class and when I saw her again I told her I had missed her. She looked at me shocked as if to say, "Why would anybody miss me?" Little acts of love began to break down the hard exterior and a friendship developed. She had heard me mention that burgundy was my favorite color and came one day to class with a hand knitted burgundy scarf for me!

Now when I see her we smile and hug. Who would have thought that an Atheist and a Christian could have become friends?

A weight evenly distributed is not as heavy. Ever carry a way too heavy purse on one shoulder for so long that you are in great pain because of it? Try putting the same contents into a backpack where there are two straps to evenly distribute the weight. Amazing difference. So it is when we allow others in our life to share the heavy burden of pain on our shoulders. If we remain open and transparent, not only do we find relief, but we can help soothe the misery of others by sharing our experiences and what we have learned. Sometimes just hearing that someone else truly does understand our pain because they have suffered through the same experience is a tremendous comfort. Sometimes we have no words of comfort to offer, but we can, by small acts of love, help carry their burden. We are consoled simply by knowing we are not alone. There were other occasions when Meesha and I thought of each other and brought a small gift or baked good to class. One day, she brought me a beautiful leather coat she no longer wore, my favorite color of course, burgundy. It was by a famous French designer, Etienne Aigner, and was made in the 80's. I was so touched! I love this coat, not only because it is a beautiful leather coat, but because it comes from Meesha. I wear it proudly, and every time I slip it onto my shoulders I think of her, and of her shoulders that must have slid into it for many years as well, and also of the heavy, sorrowful burden those shoulders bore for these many years, and it serves as a constant reminder to me to help bear the burden and pain of others.

So, there are Meeshas in the world, who remain bottled up; for her the prison door of pain remains shut. However, there are others who have chosen not only to slay the dragon of sorrow, but to take their blood stained sword and wave it high for others to see, trumpeting the fact that it can and must be done. This leads me to Michele.

Behind the Laugh Lines

MICHELE IS ANOTHER WOMAN in this class; she is 80 years old. She has raven black hair, dyed now of course, but it once was her natural color. She has piercing blue eyes. She is still strikingly beautiful *belle comme la nuit,* and has a great sense of humor. She was born in France but moved to America in her twenties. Her story is a sorrowful one yet it also holds a miracle. The opposite of Meesha, she is very open to telling her story, in fact, does so publicly at the Holocaust Museum among other places. Yes, Michele grew up in France during the time of German occupation and Hitler's gruesome concentration camps.

Michele had three older brothers. The youngest of them, Maurice, was on his way to high school one morning when German soldiers boarded the bus and told all the men to drop their pants. The French do not circumcise their boys, Jews do, and this is what the soldiers did to identify them and lead them off to the concentration camps. Maurice was

17; can you imagine how humiliated and fearful he must have felt? They never saw him again.

Michele was only 8 at the time. All Jews were forced to wear a yellow Star of David on their clothing. Branded like animals soon to be slaughtered. One day Michele was outside playing hopscotch with two of her friends who were not Jewish. Soldiers pulled up, saw her yellow star, scooped her up into a truck and drove her off to a triage camp. This is where they sorted out the sick and handicapped from the healthy and also decided who went to which camp. The unhealthy were simply shot. She was there for three months. It is unimaginable to me to be 8 yrs. old, separated from your parents and siblings, not even having the ability at that age to comprehend what was going on. Terrified, hungry, cold, mistreated for 3 insufferably long months. Then came the miracle.

Michele's oldest brother was in the French Underground, better known as the French Resistance. Like many who live in Europe, Michele's family spoke a few other languages. Her brother just happened to speak perfect German. He, by some means, Michele never wanted to ask how, obtained a German Officer's uniform. He somehow found out which camp Michele was in and donning the uniform he entered the camp. In perfect German he pointed to Michele and 2 other girls as well, so as not to arouse suspicion, and said gruffly, " I want these three, outside now!" The soldiers complied with their orders and Michele was free. However, she was not free to go home since her parents were in hiding. Instead she was taken to a convent. German soldiers often searched convents for hidden Jews so one day shortly after her arrival she was taken into the woods nearby and told to hide there until the nuns returned for her. She, at 8, was alone in those woods for 3 days. She had no food, was terribly frightened by the animal noises that echoed around her at night as thoughts swirled around in her mind of whether or not she would ever see her parents again, or if the nuns would return for her. Thank God they did return. She could not stay long though due to the frequent searches.

Her father was very well off and also had a close friend who was some sort of government official in the city. This official had their house boarded up to look like it was abandoned but her parents hid and lived in a small space in the basement. The official would sneak them food from time to time, but these were no conditions for a child. It was arranged for a family to be paid to take Michele in. She was with them for one year. According to her words, she is thankful because they saved her life, but they were awful people who treated her very poorly. She attended school but had to use a false name and learn to lie to hide her true identity. She did not know whether her parents were alive or if she would ever see them again. Finally, the war ended and Michele remembers the American soldiers rolling into the town in their tanks and throwing Juicy Fruit gum to all the children. She says to this day it is still her favorite gum. She always has some in her purse, and a never- ending supply at home because every group of school children that hears her story sends her Juicy Fruit gum.

Michele was reunited with her parents and went on to live a normal life. As normal as one can, having experienced such atrocities at such a young age. Also, living with the constant reminder of those experiences because of the permanent void in their family where her brother Maurice once was, and who was no more. Let us speak his name and never forget it so that we never again allow the horrors of evil men like Hitler to be repeated. Shout his name and remember it, Maurice Rambert, formerly Rosenberg before they changed their name, whose life was savagely ended along with 6 million other lives. Among these 6 million were 198 in Michelle's family line. Her father had 7 brothers, also with families, and so a total of 198 related or connected to Michele's family line perished in this horrific nightmare.

Somewhere through her experiences Michele learned that humor would not only lighten her own load, but also soften the hearts of others. A healing balm to be applied as often and as plentifully as possible. It didn't take long after meeting her to be the benefactor of her masterful sense of humor, and I, as a wounded soul myself, deeply appreciate it.

Michele, having grown into quite a beauty, was sought after by many young men. She is very intelligent and made the highest grades in school. However, could any amount of success or attention ever fully erase the deep wounds and scars etched on her soul? You can never forget such a horrible, painful experience, but she says what helped her to rise above it was the incredible love her family had for her.

She came to the United States in her early twenties to join her older brother who had started a business here. She met and married a man who also happened to be a survivor of the camps. She had a wonderful marriage until her husband died at 70. She has a son, and a grandson, both whom she adores. The way she is always telling jokes or making wisecracks one would never know her painful past. She is beautiful and well dressed and her remarks can sometimes seem flippant. One might mistakenly think that she has led a charmed, shallow life, but she is only doing what she has learned to do to keep the pain and over-seriousness of life at bay. Behind the laugh lines and quips is a tender-hearted, generous woman who chose to use her pain to help others. She speaks of her Holocaust experiences at the Holocaust Museum as well as schools and other various places. I have gone to hear her speak. She uses her pain as a tool to try to carve out a better future for the world and for individuals. She not only speaks everywhere about her experiences but has worked on fundraisers for the disabled and basically helps out wherever she can. She stands up for people whenever she sees injustices and encourages others to do the same. Though nothing could ever erase the horrible events of her past, I believe that each time she shares her story and brings awareness, and with each kind act or joke to lighten someone's heart and put a smile on their face, the scars on her own soul are a little less piercing and a little more bearable. She is a bottle broken open. She has slain the dragon and wields high her sword. She was not only freed from the literal prison of the Concentration Camp, but she also unlocked the prison door of pain through helping others.

Suddenly every face I encounter holds a mystery for me. Every line I hear spoken holds many more unspoken to be discovered. Behind the sorrow lines, the laugh lines, the worry lines, etc. is a story untold and a hero unsung. Society would look upon these "elderly" as useless, something to be discarded, yet there is a beauty beneath the weathered binding. Like a tattered but treasured old book of beautiful poems and stories, lying on the shelf just waiting for its pages to be turned and mysteries to be discovered.

Let us not forget the famous quote by Edmund Burke, "Those who don't know history are destined to repeat it." Why not learn from the lessons of those who have gone beyond their pain? Those who have done it right as well as those who have done it wrong, so that we do not repeat the same errors but glean from the struggles and stories of others. Listening to the history of their past serves a twofold purpose: it honors these invisible stars, unsung heroes, giving their life purpose, and it enlightens and equips us, that our life might have purpose.

Two very different women, different circumstances, different responses and outcomes. One thing remains the same—pain is a prison from which we all long to escape. For some, it is the prison of our own mind and memories, like Meesha, for others, it is a literal, physical set of walls imprisoning us, like Michele, in the Concentration Camp. There are still others who are like those who suffer with the medical condition "Locked-in Syndrome," where they are alive, yet, lifeless because they are unable to move any part of their body and so are doomed to merely watch others live from the prison of their own body. Such is the metaphor in the case of my father.

Behind the Boundary Lines

PERHAPS THE SADDEST STORY of all is that of my father. Not because his circumstances were the most painful, but because his attempt to overcome his pain was the feeblest. A non-attempt really; he chose to hide.

Arthur William Sherman, that's my father. Part Cherokee Indian, part Danish, and a few others in the mix. A good mix, he was handsome as a young man; everyone who sees a photo of him when he was young says he looked like Elvis. He did. His claim to fame was that he was once even asked for his autograph. Beneath the well-crafted exterior, however, was a broken soul that never found its healing this side of Heaven.

Outward appearances can be deceiving, not only that of my father, but also his family. They seemed to be the typical perfect American family; a father, mother, one boy and one girl. They went to church on Sundays. No one would ever suspect the wormwood at work rotting the trunk of the family tree.

I don't know at what point my father became aware of it or how long it had been going on, but, his father had been molesting his sister. A poisonous cancer that destroyed the family from the inside out. They stopped going to church. Was it because of guilt or the fear of someone finding out? How long did their mother know and keep quiet? I don't know; I only know that it continued until his sister was 16 and became fearful of getting pregnant and finally gained the courage to stand up to him. No one ever talked about it. It remained a secret for many years and I never learned of it until I was an adult and had children of my own. Looking back I could see signs that something was abnormal. For example, my grandparents had separate bedrooms. There was an unexplained tension at family gatherings like Christmas. Tension that even a child like myself at the time could pick up on but hardly be capable of deciphering or understanding such issues. For me, it was just always an uneasiness that was felt in their home. I know that I felt awkwardly uncomfortable when my grandfather hugged me, a little too tight, a little too long, and I did not like the smell of alcohol on his breath when he was close either. He drank too much. Probably a contributing factor to his abominable deeds.

It was my aunt herself who finally confided in my mother, many years later, when she was married with 3 children. I believe for her the breaking of the dam came when she had a fourth child that died. She was only about 18 months old; she drowned. After that, she was so riddled with guilt and pain that she could no longer keep up the facade, no longer even tolerate the sight of her father, so they moved away to the other side of the country. Before they did though, she opened up to my mother. She said she had once reached out to an aunt for help, finally breaking the silence and taboo of the horror that was happening, but she was told to be quiet. She was warned that it would destroy the family and bring shame to their name. She never mentioned it again. How did my father know then? He must have walked in on the act, which makes me wonder, "Was he physically threatened to never tell? Was he abused as well?" I will never know. He never spoke about it. The only acknowledgement of it that ever came from his lips was when my youngest sister heard about it after she was married. My father had not been a great father and given this information she saw him in a different light and wanted to call and thank him for not ever touching us. She told him that he actually did a great job being a father considering the monster he was raised by. He simply said, "Yes, thank you." Whether my father suffered physically or not I do not know, but I DO know he never recovered or healed emotionally. As a matter of fact, the more time that went by, the more he withdrew from life.

He fell in love with my mother in high school and they were married right after. She was pregnant with me, which hurried things along a bit, but they had planned to marry anyway. He was only 19 when I was born, my mother 18. At first things were good and they were happy. Finding love with my mother and moving into their own home must have been a haven and a respite from his inner anguish, but as more and more responsibilities came from work and having more children he caved from the pressures of life. He began to drink heavily, especially when he had to go with all of us to his parent's house. I'm sure it was full of haunting memories since they still lived in the same house. Having to keep the dirty secret weighed heavily on him and made him feel dirty. Though he committed no crime, the guilt he felt was as if he did. Children internalize everything. If anyone in your family has done something bad then you must be bad is what they tend to think. I'm sure he also lived with the guilt of not being able to protect or help his sister. Unfortunately, familial molestation is a violation that occurs too frequently in this world. So many families have been tainted by it. No one wants to talk about it, but what adds to the damage is not talking about it. Like a boiling pot with the lid on, it will eventually boil the contents over. Remove the lid and the contents will boil away and evaporate. Keeping the lid on painful secrets will cause them to boil over into all other areas of your life, and boil over into the following generations.

Growing up, I saw my father as an angry man who didn't seem to have time, love or patience for his children. He always kept himself at a distance from us kids— never affectionate. It all made sense though after knowing his past. If you don't show any affection there is no room for, or risk of any improper touching right? Maybe my father wasn't just some cold, uncaring man after all. Funny how once you know the story behind the story, once you've unearthed the skeletons buried in someone's past, you see them from a completely different angle. Not that it erased all the pain and suffering of my childhood, having a father who not only never showed any love but who was very verbally abusive, but it took the focus off me and my pain and put it on him and all that he must have endured, which allowed me to forgive him. An absolute in the healing process.

My father drank to suppress his feelings but when even that did not suffice he cut himself off more and more from society, people and all emotions. He would not go out to public places like restaurants or the beach with my mother and us; he only did what was absolutely required of him like going to work, although he would sometimes go to a bar to drink. He became nonexistent to us all, except of course when he was yelling at us. Then we were all too painfully aware of his existence. My mother could no longer handle it and they divorced when I was 16. Did this serve as a wake-up call for my father to finally deal with his demons? No. Tragically, his life continued to spiral downward, completely isolating himself by the end of his life. He tried to have other relationships after my mother, even remarrying once, though it was very short-lived. My father never learned, or never allowed himself to live and love and feel; he only knew how to play the game well enough to survive. Eventually, the facade erodes, the curtain is pulled back revealing the weak and frightened little man that portrayed himself as the great and powerful Oz. So it was with my father, and so he became a recluse. He moved in with his mother in order to take care of her in her old age and sickness. His father had died years before, with never a word breathed of admission, regret or any kind of acknowledgement. He stayed there with his mother until she passed away.

My father had tried at one point to find his sister and get in touch with her to let her know that their mother would not be alive much longer. His sister had long ago cut off all family ties. He did, in fact, track her down. She refused, even under the circumstances, to speak to her mother. There was no forgiveness, no reconciliation, no communication, not even a tirade of blame. There was only a cold, permanent silence. Old wounds were reopened and left gaping.

I myself had very little contact with my father because it just tore the wound deeper. He never called me; when I called him, after 5 minutes he would say, "Ok, well, I better let you go," which was really him saying to himself, "Don't get too close, don't feel, just self-protect." He was that way with all of us. He kept himself safely isolated behind the gated mobile home community where he had lived with his mother. Though it was on beautiful grounds with a rec room and pool and many other amenities, he called it God's waiting room. It was only the elderly that lived there and it seemed every other week someone died. Since he mentioned it often I know it weighed on him as the years went by, knowing that one day it would be his turn. To die when you have never truly lived is an awful fate. He had the choice to enter into the life and lives around him. He had children and many grandchildren, but he chose to stay at a distance. He did have a few friends, but only those in the mobile home park that he played pool with in the rec room. Towards the very end, he even shut them out. He started to have a recurring, haunting nightmare; he was outside of a house, alone in the dark, peering in a window where he could see all of us, laughing and having a great time and carrying on, unaware of his presence, and he was unable to make contact and let us know he was there. Very telling of his condition and life experience.

He became ill and quickly declined. Since he lived alone and we rarely saw him, we were not aware of his decline until it was very drastic. The last time I had seen him he looked healthy and was still sharp as ever mentally. It had been a little less than a year. Though I lived the closest to him, I lived in an apartment with just enough room for my husband and me and my youngest child still living at home. My sister Kristin lived in a big house in Iowa and had always offered for my father to come stay with her if ever he grew tired of being alone. One day she got a call from my panicked father. He had mentioned a few times before that he was concerned about blood in his stools. He finally went to the doctor, unfathomable if you knew my father; to a man afraid to go out in public places a visit to the doctor was so personally invasive that he avoided it at all cost most of his life. Unbelievably, he was misdiagnosed, they found nothing. We found out later, much too late, that he had actually been to the emergency room and the doctor twice, yet, no one detected that he had colon cancer. It was only after the panicked phone call from my father asking my sister to book him a flight to Iowa, again, so out of character for my father, how desperate he must have been, and her gasping at his appearance when she went to pick him up at the airport that he was taken to a doctor there in Iowa and properly diagnosed. My sister told me that our father was hardly recognizable, not only because of the tremendous loss of weight, but he had also aged so rapidly. A once large, sturdy man, with dark hair, though some gray in it, was now a frail, 140 pound white haired shadow.

My sister did everything humanly possible to help my father. Not an easy task. Though it seemed my father had reached out to her in an attempt to save his life there was an immediate measure of ambiguity in his actions. She had to forcibly take him to the doctor, and even after the discovery of a large tumor in his colon, he tried to refuse surgery. His actions and choices suggested that the reality of the situation was that he was not trying to save his life but was merely afraid of dying alone. What did he expect of my sister, to sit idly by and watch him deteriorate and painfully slip into eternity a broken and battered man who never really reconciled to his children or his past? No. He wasn't a good father, but neither was he the monster his father was and even if he was, should she be a monster and callously allow him to suffer thinking he deserved this kind of end? Even if some would think so, it was not in my sister to do so. It soon became clear that my father who once, and quite recently still had, a photographic memory, and was highly intelligent, was no longer in possession of his full faculties physically or mentally. He went into nonsensical rants and became rather belligerent. For this reason, my sister obtained a legal power of attorney and had the doctors proceed with the surgery. It was extremely success-ful; they removed the whole tumor and there didn't appear to be any spreading of cancer or any traces of the cancerous tumor or cells left. They didn't even think that Chemother-apy was necessary. One would, in a normal state of mind, be exuberant about such news, not my father. He was angry. He had long ago given up on life and would have preferred to die and end his suffering. From that point on, he held a grudge against my sister, either because she didn't allow him to die, or because he was no longer in charge of his own decisions, probably both. She tried to take care of him in her home after his release from the hospital but it proved to be too much. Belligerent and miserable, it took a toll on my sister's children, and my sister regressed to the emo-tional state she was in when she was a small child and had to endure the repercussions of my father's anguish. Unable to bear it any longer, she found a facility for him. It was a welcoming, caring assisted living home for the aging.

Though the grounds were beautiful, the staff friendly and helpful, and the facility full of activities and hobbies to occupy him, as well as people interested in befriending him, my father had spent so many years building the walls of a safe fortress around himself that here in this strange, new environment he panicked. The bricks of routine and famil-iarity that he used to build his fortress were now torn down and he became once again a frightened little boy. Previous to falling ill, the past several years of his life, since he could not attach himself to people, in order to try to fill the aching void he became quite the consumer, and attached himself to things. He bought everything from a brand new fiery red truck to musical instruments, or Civil War memorabilia, etc. Of course none of these things could satisfy or replace personal relationships, so here in this place, stripped of his false walls and possessions, the shell cracked and my father began to lose his mind and his health. A dismal affair to observe. He was unreachable, and we could only helplessly watch him slip away.

Living a couple thousand miles away, I felt even more helpless than my sister. The much dreaded day came when I got the call. It was June 7th, 2015, when Arthur William Sherman left this earth. He had given up and wanted to die, so much so, that even though my sister and mother were there at his bedside in the hospital, wanting to offer him some gest of comfort, he sent them away. I believe he could not let go in their presence; seeing their faces was a reminder of life, a possible reason to still hang on, and he wanted no part of it. However, this man who had long ago stopped caring about anyone or anything had one question to ask as my sister turned to go. To me, that last question was proof of the torment that accompanied him for a lifetime. Through labored breathing, he simply asked, "Has my sister passed?" His last thought was of his sister. How he must have loved and missed her in his life.

Though I mentioned before, the years with no contact, and the one failed attempt to reunite his mother and sister, many years after that there was, in fact , one last call between them. My sister Kristin had found my cousins on Facebook and started fishing and prodding to find out if their mother was interested in reconciling with my father. She was ready, and so was my father. Soon there was a tearful but joyful conversation on the phone. Since they lived in different states there had to first be a phone call before meeting face to face. They talked for hours, laughed and cried, promised to be in touch again soon, and hung up thankful to have reconnected after all those years. Neither knew at that moment that though this call was a first, it would also be their last. Re-found joy quickly turned once again to sorrow. Shortly after that call, my aunt had a severe stroke that left her not only unable to move but unable to speak. Years of unspoken words between them that were only just beginning to find their place would now never be uttered. Lost along with his sister's capacities was my father's last chance to work things out and finally put his pain to rest. I believe at that point that the last frayed thread that my father was holding onto snapped. He went into eternity, never slaying the dragon. He had lived his whole life locked behind the prison door of pain.

Between the Lines

BETWEEN THE STORY OF Meesha, Michele, and my father, is the life story I can best recount to you...my own. I can not speak of overcoming pain if I do not speak of my personal sorrow. What if the prison was your own wounded, but hardened heart that held you captive throughout your life? What if you finally found the key to unlock the prison door and walk free...free to thrive instead of just survive? This, is my story.

Having first told my father's story you will better understand my own; since my choices, situations and experiences in life were, at least in part, so directly linked to our dysfunctional relationship. I don't know if your life has been like mine, but I have had so many diverse experiences that I feel as though I have lived many lives, or at least, that my life is divided into sections. Therefore, between the lines of childhood and adulthood, between the fragmented lines that have sectioned my life, as with all people, there is a story.

I was born May 8th, 1958, and grew up in a middle-class family, in a middle-class neighborhood. From the outside, all looked well. A mother, father and four children in our house with bright white paint and neatly trimmed black contrast on the borders and shutters. As I look back now, it is a reflection of the light and darkness that was taking place in my life on the inside. In the light, there was my loving, attentive mother who zealously picked out patterns, fabric, and matching buttons to sew all our clothes for school, and who piled us all in her light blue Chevy station wagon, along with an ice chest packed with drinks and peanut butter sandwiches for a day of frolicking and lingering at the beach until sunset. As we grew up in the San Fernando Valley, a trip to the beach was quite the adventure. I can still hear the shrill of our competitive, joyful voices as the car came over the hill and we shouted, "First one to see the water!"

I remember her faithfully every morning making us hot chocolate and toast to warm our bodies and souls before sending us off to school. A warm and light memory, and even writing it now these almost 50 years later, I can feel the warmth of that blue plastic mug in my hands and smell the toast in the toaster and see my mother smiling at me as she pulled out that red plastic butter dish. Yes, the smells and sensations of home were pleasant, at least when my mother was around, but there was, unfortunately, the dark side; my father.

I have already told my father's story so you know that he was an angry, alcoholic, distant father. No need to repeat it, but what you don't yet know is how all of that affected me. Though I have found much healing, I still bear scars. Not physical scars; my father never laid a hand on me, but emotional scars, which in my opinion can sometimes be worse than physical ones. Let me explain; when someone is bruised and battered by physical abuse, at least it is obvious why you are hurting. Someone hits or slaps you; you feel immediate pain, there is a direct connection, you know the cause of your pain. With verbal abuse, as a child, you believe and internalize the negative, demeaning lies that are spewed on you. It takes many years sometimes to discover why you run from people, jobs, and any other situation where something is spoken that triggers the mechanism of fight or flight in you. I spent years thinking something was wrong with me, that I was just born with some defect of character or mind that caused me to be unable to cope with normal, everyday situations in life. I have spent a lifetime trying to overcome feeling less than others. Less able, less worthy of love or position in this world. Even after finding a relationship with the God who created me, and even after marrying a man who adores me and thinks I am beautiful, talented, and smarter than he is, the battle has raged on. Of course I have found a level of healing, and even though I continue to grow in that healing, unbelievably, after all these years, I am still sometimes haunted by my father's words whenever I attempt a new task.

My father was so lost in his own world of pain that he had no time or patience for children. I think the only time he ever spoke to us was to yell at us about something. We were always on edge when he was around, just waiting for the proverbial bomb to drop. Whose turn would it be today to endure his volatile verbiage? Phrases like, "You stupid piece of s**t", or "stupid jerk," were accompanied by a string of curse words that a child should not only never hear but definitely never have directed at them.

Seems like no great mystery to those of you reading this now why I have thought so little of myself my whole life, but when you grow up in that type of environment, since birth, and all your formative years you never knew anything else, trust me, it takes years to discover and connect the dots from your past to your present. Especially since all you want to do is forget your past. However, the echoes of its pain will surface and shout at you when you least expect it, and will continue to do so until you dare to venture back and fit the puzzle pieces together. Until then, our life is just floating pieces, beautiful as they may be, they have no framework and can not form the full beauty of the artwork our life is meant to be. We all, who have worked on puzzles, know that you must first find the edge pieces and form the framework if we are to successfully finish the picture.

One of those pieces or one of the dots I have connected is best expressed by this story and example of what it was like to eat at the table with my father. As much as weekday breakfasts of hot chocolate and toast are a warm and light memory, the memory of weekend breakfasts is a dark and frightful one. Since my father worked early during the week, weekends were the only time we all shared a meal as a family. Though we looked forward to it because it was quite a full and delicious meal; scrambled eggs, bacon, potatoes, and peanut butter and jelly on our toast instead of just butter; my father, the forever looming, dark cloud in our lives, quickly dispersed any sunshine of joy. So irritated by the normal noise and chaos of children, I am sure my father dreaded meals with us. It was apparent on his face and of course in his words. I still feel paralyzed at the memory of reaching for my glass, and my father screeching before I even made contact with the glass with my fingers, "Don't spill your milk!" In addition to the "stupid", "jerk", and varied curse words, there was the undertow of the silent message in moments like this. It evoked in me not only the fear of error but it would, for the rest of my life, announce to me every time I was about to attempt something (reach for that milk) that I assuredly WOULD make a mistake.

No one likes to fail or make a mistake, but it is a different level of fear when there is a bitter root attached to it that is so bristly and heavy that the mere reminder of it drags you down into the dark underground where it flourishes. Once you are there, it is extremely difficult to dig and claw yourself back up to the surface and its light.

Another connect the dots moment came one day after years of wondering why, always at dusk, a sudden feeling of dread and an inexplicable depression crept in so often over the course of my life. I don't remember the exact day, month, or even year of that "aha" moment, but I do know that I was already married with children of my own when this revelation came. A flashback moment played out in my head as my stomach knotted at the all too real memory of being a child, and as dusk set in, knowing that my father would soon be pulling into the driveway home from work. No matter how heartily we had all been laughing, or what exciting game we had been playing, or whatever moment of joy we might have been experiencing, like water thrown on a fire, it was instantly snuffed out by the gloomy shadow of dusk foretelling the imminent arrival of my father's presence in the home and all the unpleasantness that came with it. He never spoke a kind word, never told us he loved us. My only memories of my father speaking directly to me were either of him yelling at me (us) to be quiet and telling us to go play in our room, or screaming one of our names until we heard and fearfully came out of that room only to find that all he wanted was for us to come change the channel on the T.V. for him because he was too lazy to get up. Obviously, this was in the days before remote controls.

The fear I had of my father as a young child turned to disdain as my teenage years approached. I remember the first time I ran. I believe I was 12 or 13. I don't remember what I had done to be grounded and sent to my room by my father but I was enraged at the injustice, sure I had done nothing to warrant it. I sat there fuming for a short while; indignant that already being sentenced to a life with a father like mine, I was now being confined to these four walls. Feeling like a caged, wild animal, suddenly, I saw just outside my bedroom window the brick wall surrounding our yard and felt sure I could climb over it. As quietly as I could, I opened the window and snuck out. I made it over the wall and felt giddy as I ran down the street with a newfound sense of power pulsing through my every cell.

That first time, my freedom was short lived. Where does one go at 12 or 13? I don't remember where I wandered or how long I was gone, but the power and thrill of escape became an addiction. I had discovered that if you can't change your circumstances you can always flee from them. The problem is though physically you can run, emotionally you can not really run from pain, or your past; one day it will catch up with you and you will run right into a brick wall instead of going over it. I spent many years running before that day came, but it did come. Before I tell you about that day, let me take you on the journey that led me there as I recount some of the stories of my youth and accumulated pain.

Emotionally crippled by my formative years spent with my father, the choices I began to make as a teenager reflected my aching soul. Hungry for male approval and love, I began a life of sexual promiscuity and drugs at a very young age. By 14, I was no longer a virgin and not only smoked cigarettes but had experimented with Marijuana.

There had been joyous times in my childhood; I always had friends. I have pleasant memories of ice skating at the mall every weekend in my sixth grade days, or horseback riding with a different group of friends in Junior High years, followed by sleepovers filled with laughter; even so, there was always this undertow of sadness trying to drag me down to the depths. I could never really completely shake it off or cover it up; thus began my life of drugs. Marijuana was a thrill at first; an escape, and I loved the way it made me laugh. However, it always seemed to make me feel paranoid, so I began to experiment with other drugs to dull the gnawing pain in my heavy heart. I was longing to feel like I belonged. I had always felt like all the world had to offer was for everyone else, not for me. The roots of that feeling were not only from the mistreatment by my father, but I had heard the story of how my mother, not quite having graduated high school, found out she was pregnant with me and was so scared to death to tell her parents that she repeatedly did belly flops in the pool hoping to cause a miscarriage. Though my mother loved me once I was born, the unearthing of that story only added to the sense of rejection that I already felt from my father and caused me to feel like I had no rightful place in this world. Unworthy, unloved, and unequal to those around me, I was always searching for a place where I felt I belonged. This left me extremely vulnerable. Male attention became like a drug itself, after all, if any male was attracted to me and wanted to be with me then I must be worth something right? Though I was definitely longing to be loved, my mind and heart became twisted and men became something to conquer. Since men were usually only looking for one thing and quickly moved on to the next once the thrill was gone, I suppose I unconsciously decided to beat them at their own game. I say men, but really most of them were just boys, and who was I kidding? I was not really beating anybody at any game. I was instead gouging multiple, deeper scars into my already wounded heart and soul.

At 16, my parents divorced, which we children could not have been happier about. We rejoiced in a newfound sense of freedom from years of bondage, but, for me anyway, that freedom and joy were short lived. It was not long after the divorce that my mother met Pete. To her he was a dream come true, for me he soon became a nightmare worse than my father.

The foundation of my home life was already in shambles, due not only to the emotional destruction done by my father but also the destruction done by my own hand in opening the door to sex and drugs at a young age. The structure that remained was a fragile house of cards and Pete was the final gust that brought it crashing to the ground. I tolerated him for a while for a couple of reasons. One, because my mother seemed happy, and two because he had his cool side, giving me "Black Beauties", amphetamines, from time to time.

No "cool side" could ever make up for his obnoxious behavior though. He also turned out to be an alcoholic and had very inappropriate, crude language filled with innuendos. I always felt anxious and uncomfortable around him.

The divorce was now final and the house needed to be sold. With the end of their marriage and the end of the house I had known as my home, I thought it was also the end of Pete. He and my mother had some kind of rupture so after the house was sold we moved, without Pete, to an apartment in Granada Hills. I looked forward to this new chapter in my life; a new home, a new city, new school and a new hope. The transition was not as easy or as hopeful as

I had imagined though. If I felt before that I did not belong or fit in, it was certainly accentuated now in this new school where I definitely did NOT fit in. We begged my mother to move back to Van Nuys so we could go to school with our friends, so after a few months, we did. We found an apartment right across the street from Grant High School and I was excited to be back on familiar ground. No amount of joy ever lasted long though in my life, and this was no exception. Shortly after we moved in, Pete was back in my mother's life and moved in as well. He was more offensive than ever, and now he was also trying to take a father's role and tell me what to do. I could no longer stand the circumstances at home, and the last card of my crumbling structure fell as I packed my few things in a bag and ran away at the tender age of 16.

I had a friend whose mother had left to move in with her boyfriend, leaving her and her slightly older sister; my friend was 16 and her sister was 18, alone in their apartment. They knew of my plans to run away and had said that I could stay with them. Sounded like paradise to me. Paradise soon turned sour though with no job and no money for food. Her sister had a job, though she didn't earn much, and needed gas for her car. My friend and I dropped out of school and began searching for jobs. I remember there being one box of cereal we all shared for about a week during the roughest time. I did finally find a job at Bob's Big Boy, but with 3 young girls trying to split the rent and bills and food it was not working. I left, though I do not remember where I went at first. From that point on my memories are very clouded. My life from 16 to 21 was an endless stream of sex and drugs and moving from place to place, job to job and heartache to heartache, though it was mingled with lots of laughter with my 2 best friends. My partners in crime were Leslie and Mandie, whom I had met in Jr. High.

Blurred Lines

I HAD TWO BEST friends during my teenage years; I sometimes think they were each a side of my personality. I met them both in Jr. High. Mandie was my zany, absolutely in your face don't care rebel, with whom I always got into some kind of trouble, like the time we snuck out at night with her mother's car and crashed it into a pole. Leslie, though we certainly did some crazy, rebellious things, was one who still liked to keep things in order, and was highly intelligent. We took French together in Jr. High and High School and dreamed of a trip to France. We were studious and got an A in the class. During the wild ride of my teenage years, I vacillated between these two friends, but laughed easily and heartily with either. With all the drugs and changes of that time, I have trouble recalling some of the details, or sometimes mix up the sequence of experiences on the timeline of my life. The lines have become blurred.

I don't remember how we heard about the "Sugar

Shack", but it was a club specifically for UNDER 21. There were so many clubs for 21 and over, that someone had the "genius" idea to open a club for minors. Teenagers from all over the San Fernando Valley migrated to this fantasy watering hole. Of course they were not allowed to sell alcohol, so the bar served sodas and chips and a limited menu of food items. On the sly, however, Quaaludes and various other drugs were sold or given in abundance. If you were a pretty girl and had no money, occasionally some guy would give you a couple of Quaaludes, I'm sure with the hopes of you giving him something later on once you were under the influence. There was a large dance floor and an upstairs room with couches and pinball machines, though my friend Leslie and I spent little time up there; most of our time was on the dance floor or hoping for that next David Bowie song to come on. "Rebel, Rebel" was one of our favorites and upon hearing the first few notes, our eyes widened as we grabbed each other's hands in excitement and ran to the dance floor. Under the disco ball and strobe lights, dressed in tight jeans, midriff- baring t-shirts and platform tennis shoes, we danced all night, unless one, or both of us, had gone off with some guy for a while. Thinking now of the words to that favorite Bowie song, how true they ring: "Rebel, Rebel, you've torn your dress, Rebel, Rebel, your face is a mess, Rebel, Rebel, how could they know? Hot tramp, I love you so." We were rebels, and we were tramps, though we certainly didn't think so. We were products of the 60's and 70's; those that tried to change the world with protests, sit-ins and love-ins, and sex, drugs and rock and roll. It was all about being free to express yourself and we were no exception. At one point I even dyed my hair red and cut it like Bowie's hair on his "Pin Ups" album. Being free to choose is a wonderful thing, but not everything we choose is wonderful; sometimes what we choose leads to our own destruction.

Sometimes instead of going to the Sugar Shack we found out about some party going on at someone's house and went. Sometimes we knew the person whose home it was, most of the time we did not; we were just given an address by some friend or even friend of a friend. It didn't matter. That's just how it was back then in the Valley; someone's parents went out of town and so they threw a party. Sometimes the parents were there and didn't care. A lot of parents in the 70's smoked pot so they just joined the party. My own mother, thanks to Pete, became a pot smoker. I suppose she had felt so bound by her marriage to my father, and also by having become a mother at 18, having 2 children by 19 and 4 by 25, that after the divorce she wanted to be a little wild and free. She did some kooky things. One thing was that for some reason she bought a goat for a pet. We did not live in a farm area; we lived in a residential area of the San Fernando Valley, so why she wanted a goat in our backyard is a mystery. She thought it was cool and so did we. A few times, before my mother sold the house, my sister and I held some of those valley parties at our house and thought it would be funny to let the goat in to wander around once everyone was high. We laughed hysterically at their reactions; no one wanted to admit that they saw the goat, thinking that they were just too high and seeing things, but soon we would hear whispers among the crowd saying, "Is that a goat?" My sister, my friend Leslie and I would follow the goat around but stand nonchalantly close by pretending to have a conversation while secretly watching and listening for people's reactions, and we would laugh until we cried. It was quite the entertainment...until the goat starting pooping its pellets on the carpet and we had to clean it up.

The valley parties continued for years; the days of the Sugar Shack, though they seemed to have gone on for years, were really just one long summer that continued a bit into the Fall. That period of my life so impacted me and is so full of memories that it is difficult for me to believe that it lasted such a short time. In fact, it is only a recent revelation while trying to reconstruct the timeline of my life that I discovered how short a time it actually was. During that time, I wound up staying at Leslie's house for a month or two. After having run away, and after leaving the 2 sisters' house, though I don't know where I went directly after that, I do know that eventually Leslie's mother felt sorry for me and let me stay for a while. Leslie and I were inseparable then. We shared clothes and food and swapped stories of our escapades with boys (the only time we did spend apart) as we planned out what we would wear to go out that night and where or how we would get our Quaaludes. We still dreamed of France "someday" but our current passion was David Bowie. Countless nights of music, dancing, laughter and boys drowned out any sorrow or pain. I think we both felt on top of the world and a bit invincible. We were the dynamic duo.

Summer was coming to an end, and though I had dropped out of school, Leslie had continued and would be starting the new school year soon. Her mother thought that it was time for me to move back home and try to work things out with my mother and Pete. I did not want to be back under the same roof with Pete, however, they had moved from the apartment into a house and there was a little back guest house next door that had become available to rent for cheap, so my sister and I, longing for independence, moved in. She was working at a fish n' chips shop and I found a job once again at another Bob's Big Boy restaurant. This is where the lines really blur and memories are hazy. I lived in about 4 different places during a year's time, and so the events, the where and the with whom is all intermingled.

As if all the drugs and the physical displacements weren't enough to cloud my memory and cause a mental block, there was one incident that happened at age 17 that I spent years trying to forget. Like a cancerous tumor with its tentacles branched out, in trying to block out this one memory, other surrounding ones were affected in the process.

For that reason, I am not sure where I was living at the time; the little back house with Dori was no more, probably because I couldn't keep a job for long. Running away when things got unpleasant had become my habit. Anyway, I believe I was staying with my friend Mandie and her sister. I came to the house on Hazelhurst one day to see my mother. She was not home but Pete was. He said she had just gone to the store and would be back soon so I was welcome to wait. I was sitting on the couch watching T.V. when suddenly I was shocked by a very cold liquid pouring over me, down my shirt and onto my jeans. The odor told me that it was beer, and turning to see where the source was coming from, I saw Pete standing above me behind the couch, snickering as he poured his can of beer on me. At first, I thought that in a drunken stupor he had been just passing by and stumbled, accidentally spilling his beer on me, but it soon became obvious that he had done it on purpose. I was furious. He started apologizing and said that he would wash my clothes. He told me to go take a shower and put on my mother's robe while he threw my clothes in the washing machine. I should have just left at that point but I was still young and naive. I jumped in the shower unsuspectingly. After a few minutes, I thought I heard a noise in the bathroom so I turned off the water for a moment. Hearing nothing now, I started the shower again. My eyes were closed so I saw nothing, but in an abrupt flash the shower door burst open and an arm was pulling me out of the shower. Screaming and wrestling to free myself I was dragged down the hall to the bedroom.

I told no one for about a year. How could I break my mother's heart? I foolishly kept it inside as if that would make it not real; as if it never happened. Of course I couldn't make it disappear and I was tormented by this unspoken violation. Finally, one day while speaking with my sister

Dori, it spilled out. She was shocked and asked if I had told my mother. When I said no, she said that I most certainly needed to and furthermore that if I didn't tell she would. Did she? Did I write a letter? Anyway, my mother was informed. I think she could not let herself believe it, even though she raised me and knew I would never lie about such a thing. She loved him and so her heart simply could not accept it. It was brought into the open and spoken of once; neither one of us ever wanted to approach the subject again; it was too painful for us both. Little did I know until many, many years later what my mother had concluded. I assume because of my drug use and the fact that drugs alter your physical and mental state, she was able to be convinced by Pete, whose defense was that it had been consensual. It came up in a conversation with my sister decades later and I was stunned to learn what she had believed all that time. Some people would try to define or even justify rape. Is it not rape because you finally stop struggling so it won't hurt? Is it not rape when you don't go to the police? When you are forced to have sex against your will it is rape, plain and simple. Whatever my mother chose to believe about it, wasn't it enough to make her leave him? Who in their right mind would want to stay with a man who raped or had sex with her daughter? Not surprisingly, this caused a rift between my mother and me for quite some time. I rarely spoke to her during the immediate years after that.

Sadly, that was the first of three rapes in my life. Had I become a magnet for this act? The other two rapes were by strangers. When one leads a life of drugs with questionable people, you put yourself in erroneous situations. As I said before, it is all very blurred. I know that I spent time with my other best friend Mandie. I know that I continued to go to the Sugar Shack for a time with Leslie. I stayed with Mandie and her sister at their apartment for a short time, bounced around a couple of other places, eventually, believe it or not, wound up living with my father for a few years. My mother, never having worked before the divorce, had a job but was not earning quite enough to take care of my siblings. My father was not going to give my mother any more money as long as she was living with Pete, so the only solution was that my father rented a house so he could take care of them. Simultaneously, I had run out of options as far as places to stay. I don't remember how it came about but somehow the offer must have been made for me to move in as well. Having no other choice, I did.

I think by the time I moved in with my father I had turned 18. I know that my Sugar Shack adventures carried on for a while after that because I have a vivid, semi-comical memory of Leslie and I hiding two guys in my closet one night after returning from the Sugar Shack. Unfortunately, my father's bedroom was right next to the front door. We thought we were being so quiet and sneaky, but obviously, my father had heard us come in because within minutes I heard his footsteps coming down the hall. My heart almost jumped out of my chest and all of us panicked; we knew there was no quick escape and that in a matter of seconds, my father would be in the room. I think one of the guys dashed into the closet and, like sheep to the slaughter, we all followed him in. Did we really think he wouldn't look there? Did we think he would just assume he had imagined that he had heard something and walk away? It was obvious that he had not only heard us come in, but that he had heard our conversation because one of the guys had the nickname of "Frog", and as my father slid open the closet door, he screeched, "Who the heck is Frog?" It wasn't funny right then; we were petrified. When my father commanded them to get the #*@*% out, I think they were so relieved that he didn't punch them that they took off running as fast as they could. Nobody laughed then, but Leslie and I sure laughed about it in the following days, and I still laugh now these some 40 years later every time the memory resurfaces.

That is one of the last memories I have of laughing with Leslie. With her back at school, our paths began to drift and separate. I spent a lot more time with Mandie then, and also with a group of young people in my neighborhood. Floundering, a bit heartbroken and lost without my partner Leslie, I fell deeper into drugs of all kinds since they were readily available to me with this new group of people. My life became a lot more grim with heavy and frequent drug use and sleeping around still searching for love. Married men, single men, young, old; I did not acquire the fulfillment of love but the vacuity of 4 abortions. At some point, I became convinced that if I was thinner I would be more attractive and perhaps be worthy enough to find that perfect, enduring love, or at least be better accepted by the world. That led to months of being anorexic. Though I started starving myself to lose weight, what became addicting was the power I felt. My life was so chaotic and I could not change or control any of it. However, I had complete power over my own body and discovered a new way of running away by controlling my weight. My pain and circumstances wouldn't disappear, so I guess subliminally I was making myself disappear. Though I was ever searching for happiness, I was oblivious to the fact that I was heading in the wrong direction; digging a deeper and deeper pit into which I was about to fall, and almost be buried in.

Through Mandie's older sister, we had met some pretty seedy characters. Though we lived in the Valley, these "characters" lived in Hollywood. By now we had driver's licenses and would always find a car or a way over the hill to party with them. Our carryings-on with these new, so-called friends, made the craziness and imprudent behavior of our life hitherto seem like child's play. Now we were hanging out with not only drug takers, but drug dealers and the stakes were raised. There were many hair-raising episodes with these shady people, but the two that stand out most in my mind are these: the most frightful event that happened is one that, thank God, we were not part of but only heard the gory details as it was bragged about by two of the shadiest. Some guy had cheated them in a drug deal; they hunted him down and beat him so badly that they felt they had to shoot him to put him out of his misery. To my knowledge, they were never caught. The second event, unfortunately, we were privy to. For a short time, Mandie's sister had a boyfriend who was a heroin dealer. This was a serious drug, which brought serious revenue, and so drastic measures were taken to protect both. He had a gun. One day Mandie and I accompanied her sister to his house and while we were there a "customer" came to make a purchase. The boyfriend was anticipating his client's arrival and so he had taken out the small footlocker containing the heroin, and his gun. For some reason, sometime during the transaction, the boyfriend needed to leave the room and handed the gun to Mandie's sister to hold. I guess he assumed that she understood the gravity of the situation and that heroin addicts are known thieves; thus the gun to prevent him running off with the heroin and/or the money. Apparently she didn't. Mandie, curious, asked to see the gun, and her sister handed it to her. This "customer" started asking questions about the gun; what kind it was, etc., conversing and casually acting only interested in checking out this cool gun, he persuaded Mandie to hand it to him. The exact details after that I can not tell you because, by some act of God, just before she did this, nature called and I had gone to the bathroom to relieve myself. Just when I was about to exit, her sister pushed me back into the bathroom and came in as well. Without a word, she headed to the window and tried to climb out. I asked her what the heck she was doing but it fell on deaf ears at first. I started to shout it again, but she came, and with shaking hands, put her hand over my mouth. I looked up into her face, gone completely white, and wild eyes and knew there was trouble. She mumbled a few words that revealed the situation to me and then we both attempted to go out the window. After a few minutes, Mandie pounded on the door, which we tried to ignore, but she somehow got it open and angrily asked her sister why she had run off and left her alone. By some miracle, the guy had not shot anyone, however; he did run off with the gun and all the heroin. I don't remember how or when we left, but I know we were fearful of her boyfriend and any repercussions of his anger over his loss, and the foolishness of the gun being handed to this stranger. This was one of many miraculous escapes in my life.

Once, on another occasion while visiting my mother at the Hazelhurst house, before the rape ever happened, I ran to the grocery store to pick something up, and as I walked in there was a man with a gun robbing the liquor department. In that store, they had a wall safe directly behind the liquor counter, which was perpendicular to the sliding glass doors of the entrance where I had just come in. As the doors slid open, I don't know who was more fearful; me or the thief. I was stunned and afraid of being shot; he panicked, probably fearful of getting caught. Thank God he did not, by reflex, shoot blindly at me, instead, he grabbed me and threw me into the store to get me out of the way. I learned in that instant what the expression scared spitless meant as I wandered down the aisles lobotomized by fear. I hardly knew where I was, let alone what I came there for. Slowly regaining some consciousness, I started to notice other people on the aisles and wondered why they were acting so normal. Did they not know what was going on? I concluded that they must not and wondered if I should tell a worker there, but decided against it; afraid of consequences. I managed to suddenly remember what I had come there to buy; grabbed it and made my way to the register. It appeared that no one knew what was going on in the liquor department. When I got back to the house, still shaking inside, Pete said, "What the heck happened to you? You are white as a ghost!" No wonder people in the market had been looking at me so strangely! If I still had all the blood drained from my face by the time it took me to make my purchase and drive home, imagine what I had looked like while still in the store!

There were other, less daunting though still life-threatening escapades with Mandie as well. With our heavy and frequent drug use, Mandie had started occasionally having seizures. She once had a seizure while we were driving on the freeway. Thankfully, she was not the one driving, I was, but her arms were flailing and she momentarily had grabbed onto the steering wheel. A terrifying few moments as I somehow pried her hands off and redirected the car. I made it to the next off-ramp and by that time she was coming out of it.

In the same way that Leslie going back to school caused our paths to divert, there were two elements that caused Mandie and I to go down different and separate paths.

Before I begin this part of my story, I must say that it is not my intent to offend anyone or debate theology; I am simply recounting my experience. It is such an integral part of my life and story that I can not leave it out. If you were to tell me your story, I would not judge, but simply and open-heartedly accept it and only be interested in what made you who you are. All I ask is the same respect. With that said, here is the story of the first element.

After a three-day drug spree of alternating Angel Dust, Quaaludes, Cocaine and who knows what else, Mandie, her cousin and I woke up on a weekend morning and went to a swap meet where her cousin was to have a booth selling clothes I believe it was. It was a sweltering summer day, and I began to feel like my brain was frying from the outside as well as the inside, due to the drugs and the unbearable weather. Her cousin sent me to the refreshment stand to get us all drinks, but standing there in line, people swarming all around, I lost it. I couldn't seem to talk or remember why I was there. The effects of the accumulated drugs combined with the heat were beginning to take its toll. I grabbed some cokes and somehow made it back to the booth, but spiraled downward from there. I felt like I was dying, but I was so far gone that I was no longer even able to speak and ask for help. I stumbled off to the car, thinking to myself, "Well, Dawn,...you have really done it this time. Now you are going to die. It's too late, you can't even communicate with your friends to get help, this is it." Honestly, at that point, I didn't even care if I died. My life was a miserable mess. In my eyes, I was a pathetic waste of flesh; a failure, unlovable wretch, full of anger and pain. Reaching the car, I crawled into the back seat and lay down, resolved to die.

Lying there, suddenly flashing through my mind were memories of scenarios where people had been telling me about Jesus. One such memory was of walking through a park where a group of young people were preaching that

Jesus was the answer. I sneered as I passed, calling them Jesus freaks. Somehow, lying here now, I did not feel like sneering, but instead their words seemed to cut to the heart. I suddenly did not want to die and cried out, "Jesus, if you are real, I do not want to die." What happened next is quite miraculous, and I'm sure will be disputed by many, but I tell you it is the undeniable truth. I looked up at the sun and shining out from it was a brilliant, giant cross, as if the sun itself had turned into a cross. I felt a surge of peace flow through me, and though I had three days worth of drugs in me, I all at once felt none of the effects of them, and also no longer felt like I was going to die. Of course, I thought this could not be happening, that I must be hallucinating or something, so I looked away, back down at the car seat. I once again feared I was dying as my head spun and heart pounded, so I turned to look again at the sun. The cross, beaming still in its glorious radiance, once again brought peace to my soul and body. Not only did I have hope, but I began to hear a faint, inner whisper of words that were not my own. Today, I believe it to be the voice of God. I continued to turn away in disbelief and then turn back again toward this luminous cross several times before telling myself that whether this was real or not, whenever I looked at the cross I did not feel like I was dying, but instead felt peace, and so I decided to stay fixed on it. I don't know how many minutes I spent like that, I only know how I felt afterward; like I had been washed clean of every impurity in my life. I felt new, and I felt whole.

I was again speechless, but this time not by the effects

of drugs, but by the mind- boggling experience I had just had. How in the world could I explain to my friend what had just happened? I couldn't, and so on the ride home, I sat in silence. With a peace in my heart and a smile on my face, I looked out the window pondering this new discovery. For me, from that point on, no one could ever tell me that God did not exist. If I had only been hallucinating, then how is it that I am still alive and in my right mind? Can a hallucination do that? I say no. I was changed and it was immediately apparent. My whole countenance had changed and Mandie and her cousin were eyeing me strangely. They knew something had happened to me but could not begin to imagine what so they simply asked if I was ok. I was trying to make sense of it myself and could not possibly find the words to explain. Besides, I did not want to interrupt or dispel the wonder I was experiencing by debasing it with my words, so I simply nodded.

I did not grow up with any religion. My mother was Jewish, my father Protestant, but neither practiced their faith, it was just what was in their family line. I remember having asked questions about God as a young child such as, "Is God Jewish or Protestant?" but my answer was always a mere shrug of the shoulders as if to say, "I don't know and I don't care." So what was I to do now with this experience I did not fully understand? I had never been to church, never read or even seen the Bible; all I knew now was that when I felt like I was dying from my drug binge, I cried out to Jesus and immediately had a miraculous encounter and was instantaneously delivered from drugs. From that day forward I had no desire for drugs again. I could not erase from my mind or heart that illuminated cross in the sky, or the peace that had pulsed through my every cell.

A Comforting Fantasy[*]

My most secret and ultimate fantasy of all
That would conquer my troubles big and small
Would be for me to fall endlessly
Into arms so huge they could cradle the sea

Arms so strong yet so lovingly tender
They could rock the whole world
And quietly make it surrender

These arms could easily make me forget
All my troubles past and those that aren't yet
Just a few moments in this embrace
Could conquer all my fears and cause each confused
        thought to erase

Oh what I'd give to cry hearty and loud
Till my lack of confidence turned to feelings so strong and
        proud
If these arms became a reality
Then, alas, I'd live free through eternity!

---

[*]   written in March, 1979, just before my experience with God.
Surprisingly, I did not realize that it was God I was crying out for
during the writing of this poem until after my experience.

I enjoyed this newfound peace for a time as I tried to make sense of it all. God, the Bible, church, it was all so foreign to me, and I knew no one to turn to that could enlighten me or even explain what had happened to me. I did not own a Bible and finding and going to a church was still a scary thought. This is where Terry entered the scene. Have you ever heard the expression "A wolf in sheep's clothing"?

My experience had not yet distanced me completely from Mandie, so one sunny day, I was at her house and we were sunbathing in the backyard. Her sister had met a young taxi driver named Terry and had invited him to the house. He was 6'2" and had blond hair and blue eyes, quite attractive, but at this point in my life, because of my past and my spiritual encounter, I wanted nothing to do with men. Terry had wandered out into the backyard and kept trying to make conversation with me. I kept responding with curt one-word answers, trying to show that I was not only not interested, but annoyed with his chatter and attention. He didn't take the hint, and so I decided to leave. However, when I announced to Mandie that I was leaving, Terry, being a taxi driver, offered me a ride. I did not have a car at that time and so I decided to take the ride; reasoning that at least once he dropped me off I would be rid of him. Arriving in front of my house, as I reached for the door handle, he asked if he could just give me a quick kiss goodbye. Thinking he meant a brief peck on the cheek, and not wanting to seem ungrateful for the ride home, I said yes. Instead of a peck he wrapped his arms around me and planted a passionate, full-bodied kiss on my lips. Though my brain had wanted and intended to resist; something unearthly transpired between us, and I succumbed. I don't know what was emitted in that kiss but when Terry, who had gotten my number from Mandie, called the next day, though I was still reluctant, he was able to talk me into meeting him. As the saying goes, "The rest is history."

I will not belabor ALL the sordid details of the misguided and unsound relationship that continued intermittently for the next three years; but I will tell you some key facts pertaining to the subject and purpose of this book.

Between Terry's lines of professed, undying love were lies. I think even from the very beginning he was sleeping with other girls. I was either very gullible or very blindly in love. Even when I would find other girls' phone numbers in his pocket, I would swallow his stories such as; he was thinking of buying a used car from her, etc.

It was an adventure, however, and my time and travels with Terry took me to Chelan, Washington where we worked for a season on an apple orchard. It was a beautiful place, a fifty-five mile long lake, Lake Chelan, surrounded on all sides by orchards. It was in standing at the very end of the lake one day, looking up toward the other end where majestic purple tinted mountains stood, that I visually and soulfully understood the words to the song, "My Country Tis' of Thee". The words resonated in my head… "For purple mountains majesty above the fruited plains." I got it! I was looking at purple mountains surrounded by fruit-filled orchards! The scene was so imperial that it was like a sign that God was with me and for me, even in the midst of my turbulent relationship with Terry. Out of all the orchards around, the one we wound up working on was Beebe Orchards. We arrived penniless and had no food while we waited for our first paycheck, but there was an abundance of apples. By the time we got paid I thought I would never again be able to eat another apple. In fact, I didn't for many years.

The Orchard was run by a Christian man who took us to church a couple of times and I borrowed a Bible from there. When we first arrived at the orchard it was not yet harvest time for picking, so there was only work for Terry to do some irrigating. I had nothing to do while he worked, so I read the Bible. This was quite a new experience since I had never even seen one before. As I read, I started to feel a stirring in me and hear a familiar inner voice; the same I had heard the day I had seen the vision.

Terry and I became more and more diametrically opposed. When I first met him he talked about God and even recounted parts of the Bible. I was enthralled because I had never heard any of it. It was not evident until later on that he was only repeating what he had heard from his mother and stepfather and had never had a spiritual encounter himself. In fact, his life was far from anyone's idea of spiritual. To him, life was just one big party; indulging in drugs and sex whenever possible. It didn't matter what kind of drug or which girl; whatever was available. Of course, I was not aware of all this in the beginning.

The way he lived his life had put us in some perilous

situations. We had nothing, no car, no money. He quit or had been fired from his taxi driver job; I never knew the real truth with Terry. We decided to hitchhike to Washington to pick apples because it appeared to be a tremendous adventure and we had heard it brought excellent money. We packed what little clothes we had in a large backpack, bought a tent, and headed north. Along the way, hitchhiking, having no money, we were extremely vulnerable. Though we did meet some kind people that helped us, we also had some harrowing experiences as well. One of the kind ones was a mailman who was a single father of two young boys and lived just below San Francisco. He had picked us up one cold night; though it was summer, it was cold that night by the bay, and he had his heater on. We were weary from hitchhiking all day and had not eaten, so though we engaged in conversation at first, finally warm and comfortable, unknowingly, we fell asleep. I suppose he felt sorry for us, maybe he had once been in similar circumstances, so instead of waking us to drop us off when he got as far as he was going, he drove us to his home and took us in. In the morning, he had gone to work but left some food out for us along with a note and some money. Trying to repay him somehow for his kindness, I left behind my beloved Dingo cowboy boots, thinking one of his sons could use them, then we were once again on our way. Not everyone is so kind; he was a rarity. More often than not we came across those that wanted to take advantage of us in one way or another. Some, travelers like us, wanted to steal what little we had, others wanted to offer food and shelter in exchange for sex. One of the most frightening encounters, not long after, and in great contrast to the mailman, was in San Francisco. We pitched our tent at night when out in the countryside, but here in the city it was not possible, so we needed a place to stay. Some guy that Terry had partied with in L.A. had given him his phone number and said, "If you are ever in San Francisco give me a call." He did. He was excited to hear from Terry and told him they were having a party that night and we were welcome to come and stay the night. I was not fearful meeting him, but as the night rolled on and people started arriving for the "party", alarms were going off in my head and I wanted to run. Everyone was so dark; dressed in all black, sullen and eerie, they gathered around the kitchen table to dole out and snort their cocaine. I grew more and more uncomfortable as they all glanced at me so suspiciously. I wandered into another room where there were bookshelves and a small couch and I felt safer as I sat there alone. Terry came and found me and I begged him to leave but he thought I was crazy for being afraid. Soon after, his friend came in and informed me that all the others were suddenly suspicious that I might be an under-cover narc (narcotics police agent), since I had not indulged in the cocaine, and had slipped away without a word. After that, they insisted that we accompany them to this under-ground club. It was literally underground, as well as being private and secret. If I thought the others had looked at me suspiciously, there are no words for the glaring looks I was getting now. I definitely stood out in this place of wall to wall black garb. Between the ghastly crowd, the macabre, evil sounding music, the foreboding decor and atmosphere and the sheer terror running through my veins, I felt, in this place, I had truly looked the devil himself in the face. Even Terry's friend, who seemed like a dark soul himself, must have felt uncomfortable there because we did not stay long at all. Thank God. We returned to his apartment and were able to sleep, though with trepidation. The next morning, I could not wait to leave, however; his friend was still not convinced that I was not a narc, and threatened that he and his friends would not let us leave until I did a line of cocaine with them to prove I was not a cop. I feared for my life and desperately wanted to leave, so even though I wasn't convinced that they would let us leave even if I did do it, I took the chance. Surprisingly, he was satisfied and we were free to go. I have never been so happy to leave a place in my life.

As we walked down the road to the freeway to continue our trek to Washington, with the warmth and light of the sun shining on my face, I was thankful to be alive, and to be free of the horrors of the previous day. Even Terry, who when I first urged him to leave this place, shrugged it off and was only interested in getting high, admitted now that he was glad to have made it out alive.

We stuck out our thumbs and continued on our route, but before reaching our destination of Washington, we encountered some other, less than reputable people. As I mentioned before, those that wanted sexual favors in exchange for food or shelter. They had been devious about it though, pretending to be simply kindhearted people, they invited us into their home and fed us, then let us know what they expected in return. We did not accept their offer but hightailed it out of there, preferring our tent on the hard ground alone to a plush bed shared with strangers.

One day, once we were situated on Beebe Orchards, Terry took me along for the ride as he set out to rotate the irrigation pipes. Lying on the ground, on one of the rows of trees, were two men. It did not appear to be unusual at first; in this area there were many transient people called fruit tramps, people looking for work on the orchards, however, it struck us as extremely odd that when we offered to give them a ride in the jeep up to the boss's house to ask for work, they declined, stating that they preferred to walk . It was quite a distance up the hill to his house, so this puzzled us, and further causing us to be leery of their intentions was the fact that one of them never got up off the ground to greet us or engage in conversation. One of them was quite young, the one who did get up to talk to us; the other appeared to be in his thirties or forties, and never stood or smiled, but instead remained lying on the ground on top of some jackets and he acted anxiously. Though the scene was strange, Terry had to get on with his work so he dropped me off at our cabin and continued on to finish up the irrigating. I started to make breakfast and put the radio on to keep me company. The music was suddenly interrupted by a news flash. At first, I didn't pay much attention to what was being said, but quickly my ears caught a few words… "escaped convicts…one in his forties…the other just eighteen…M22 rifle…sawed off shotgun," they went on to describe them and also which area they had last been seen. These were undoubtedly the two men we had seen! I realized now why the older one had never gotten up off the ground, and what must have been under those jackets he had been lying on. I dashed out to find Terry or the boss or anybody! I think at first they thought I was crazy, but as I described what had been described on the radio the boss decided to call the authorities. The orchard was soon covered with bullet proof vest wearing officers. We later found out that they had stolen a car to escape and that the police had chased them all the way into the next state. The convicts were driving so fast that their car flipped and rolled, killing them both. It was very distressing to hear; though the older man was a hardened criminal who had been in and out of prison multiple times, the younger one, only eighteen, had a minor first-time offense, and would have been released in a short time.

This triggered in me a long reflection of all the times in my life I almost died or could have died or was at least in circumstances where it was a possibility. The three-day drug binge, Mandie's seizure while we were driving, the heroin theft, walking into a robbery at the market, numerous car accidents due to drugs and driving, the satanic San Francisco crowd, and now the convicts who could have easily shot us and stolen the jeep. There was also the time I actually came the closest to death and is the hardest to talk about.

As I mentioned previously, my relationship had been intermittent with Terry. Once, while I was still living at my father's house, and our relationship was fairly new, Terry came to my window late one night to inform me that he was going back to his ex-wife. Heartbroken hardly describes what I felt. Devastated, void of any reason to go on, I could not control the involuntary sobs emanating from my body. My wailing woke my father, and instead of what a loving, concerned father would do upon seeing his daughter in such a state; marched in and furiously screamed at me to shut up because I was waking up the whole house. Then he stormed back to his bedroom; never asked why I was crying. My heart had already just been ripped out, now my father had just stomped on it, adding insult to injury. Heart left bleeding, trying desperately not to cry, all I wanted now was to end the pain once and for all. I had been sharing a room with my little sister, who was now awake as well, so I waited for her to fall back asleep. She had seen how distraught I was and did not want to leave me alone. I assured her that I would be alright and that she should sleep. When I was absolutely sure that she was in a deep sleep, I crept quietly down the hall and into my brother's room. He was out for the night, and hidden in his room was a lockedchest of pills. He had been selling drugs. I broke open the lock and grabbed a handful of barbiturates, swallowing quickly as many as I could. I slowly made my way back to my bedroom and sat on the edge of the bed waiting for the drugs to take their effect on me. I didn't think that there was anything left in the world to make me want to stay, but after a few minutes, I looked over at my little sister in her bed and for the first time, instead of thinking about myself, I realized what this would do to her. With tears in my eyes, I softly whispered, "Good-bye Kristin." It was not humanly possible for her to have heard a slight whisper across the room while she was sound asleep; God must have intervened, because quite abruptly she sat straight up in her bed, looked at me, then without a word, ran to my father's room and announced, "Dawn took pills!" How could she have known? I made no mention of it earlier. She knew I was distraught, but I never uttered a word about pills, or desiring to end my life; I had kept it to myself. In a matter of seconds my father was in the room. He dragged me down the hall to the bathroom and yelled at me to stick my fingers down my throat so that I would throw up the pills. I defiantly, tearfully shook my head no. Against my will, they took me to the hospital. I don't remember the ride there, but I do remember being at the hospital sitting on a bench in the waiting room and a nurse asking me if I thought I would be able to stand. I nodded yes, but as I tried to stand my knees buckled and I fell to the ground. That's the last thing I remember. When I awoke, there were tubes down my nose and I was throwing up a black, tar like substance. I guess it is standard procedure after a suicide attempt to keep the patient for psychiatric observation, so I was kept there for a few days. Unbelievable that I would go back to Terry after that, but I did. He had only stayed with his ex-wife a few days before hunting me down again.

Reflecting on all these times, all these episodes where death loomed, yet; I survived, it was evident that God had spared me for a reason. Not all of those I knew during that period of my life survived. Drugs were at the root of the demise of many. One of my partying friends from the neighborhood, that I always had a crush on, died in a motorcycle accident, another neighbor, while high, dove into shallow water and was paralyzed from the waist down, another one of the group, a girl, wound up with some time in prison, a brother and sister from the Sugar Shack crowd hitchhiked to Las Vegas and were found murdered in the desert of Barstow. On and on it goes...why was I spared?

You might wonder how I could have been with someone like Terry after having had that spiritual encounter and no longer doing drugs, and him with his partying and cheating ways, but his lies were well crafted and he had an undeniable charm. It was as if I was under a spell. Now, the veneer was being stripped day by day. I hung on for a while longer, but shortly after harvest season ended, so did the relationship.

We took our earnings and bought tickets for a Greyhound Bus heading for Florida. It takes quite some time to get from Washington to Florida by bus, stopping in several cities and crossing many states. One stop, in St. Louis, Missouri, changed everything. Terry had always lied and tried to hide his flings with other girls, but this time, it was overt. He eyed an attractive young girl with bobbed auburn hair who looked a bit lost and began openly flirting with her. Of course, his story was that he was helping her find her way, however, when we all boarded the bus he went and sat down next to her! After some time passed, fuming with the indignity of it all, I walked to the back of the bus where they were seated and slapped her across the face, then returned to my seat. Why did I slap her and not him? The spell still at work I suppose. Minutes after, he came to tell me that he would not be continuing to Florida with me, but would be getting off with her at the next stop; which he did.

I stayed on the bus and continued on the route to Florida for a time, simply because I was still reeling from this gut-wrenching betrayal, and was too dumbfounded to know what else to do at this point. Staring mindlessly out of the window for who knows how many miles; aching turned to outrage. Not having any idea where to go now, since I knew no one in Florida; defeated, I decided there was no place to go but home to California, but where? Certainly not to my father, and there were no friends left to turn to; I surmised that my only hope was that my mother and Pete were on the outs again and I might stay with her for a while. Though we never again spoke of the rape after that first revealing of it, I had silently forgiven her because I loved her.

I had no money and so when I got off the bus at the next station, which was in Tennessee, I asked at the counter if it was possible since I already paid for a ticket all the way to Florida, if I could I use it to go the opposite direction to California. No such luck. Penniless, helpless, I had no choice but to hitchhike home. I took all of Terry's clothes, which were still in our common backpack, and which he had not thought to get before leaving, and threw them in the trash. This act was not only to physically lighten my load, but it was also a symbolic gesture of ridding myself of all the emotional baggage I had been carrying far too long.

Once again, God must have been with me. It is terribly

dangerous for a girl hitchhiking alone on a long trip from Tennessee to California, but my first ride was a big rig truck driver, who when he got as far as he was going, got on his CB radio and called to other drivers to give his location and ask if anyone was in the area and heading further towards California. Within minutes, another truck pulled up, and when he got to his final destination, he did the same thing. I never stuck my thumb out again and a total of 5 truck drivers drove me all the way to my mother's front door!

I was allowed to stay with my mother for a while, but Pete was once again in the picture and it was too awkward. I found a job at a cleaners and had earned a small amount of money when I learned that my sister Dori had flown to Maui for a vacation. I got the wild and reckless idea in my head to purchase a one-way ticket there to surprise her. Running, once again. I figured I could just find a small job on Maui to earn enough money for the return ticket home. With just an address of the person she was staying with scribbled on a piece of paper, off I went. Madness ensued, most of which is not worth repeating. It suffices to say that my sister was surprised and glad to see me; we had some good times, and we did make it home alive, together.

From that point in my life, again, there is a lapse of memory. Terry had been a diversion from the spirituality that had been curiously evoked in me. I still had not received any instruction; all I knew of God was experiential. There were only those few times of going to church with the apple orchard boss in Chelan, where I had been stirred enough to want to read the Bible. Now, with Terry gone, I began to feel drawn once again to the spiritual side calling within me. The lapse of memory is that I don't remember where I lived after returning from Maui, or what intermediate string of jobs I had before winding up at Biff's Restaurant in Santa Monica. I also don't remember how I first heard of the Vineyard Church, but I started attending there. My knowledge of God and how I should live my life was growing, and I was finally keeping a job and not running. I rented a little studio apartment and was independent, content, and doing well in life for the first time. After living there for only a few months, I received a phone call from Terry, who I had not heard from since the Greyhound Bus catastrophe. I don't know how he found me or got my phone number but he was crying and pleading with me; I was not having any of it. He called often for about a week, professing to be a changed man and that he wanted to come to California and start going to church with me. Feeling like a good-hearted Christian these days, I thought I should at least try to help him to do this; after all, he was someone I had once cared about. He arrived, and sadly I was once again bitten by this poisonous viper! It didn't take long though, a couple of weeks, to realize my error; I guess I had some newfound spiritual strength, and I kicked him out, this time for good.

I was back on track now and more confident than ever, however; I began to feel nauseous and tired. Yep...I soon discovered I was pregnant. I had already had four abortions in my life, and I had developed convictions about it being wrong, not only because of knowledge gained from church, but also because I had recurring nightmares of running from police, being wanted for murder, but swearing I didn't kill anyone, then opening my purse to get something and finding a dead baby inside. Therefore, for me, abortion was absolutely out of the question, even though everyone I knew insisted it was my only option since I was alone. I had one friend, Sylvia, who worked with me at Biff's that encouraged me to keep the baby and said that she would help me. When I could no longer work I moved in with her. On Dec. 5th, 1981, at 10:57 p.m., I gave birth to a perfect baby boy who I named Austin, and who changed my life forever. His due date had been Dec. 15th; sometime in late November I had a vivid dream that I was in the hospital having the baby and I saw on the wall a large calendar with a bright red circle around Dec. 5th. I remember telling my mother about it but she said it was probably just wishful thinking since I was so impatiently hoping for an early delivery. She was shocked when I called her just before midnight Dec. 4th to tell her that my water broke and I was on my way to the hospital. Austin was born just shy of 24 hrs. later, on Dec. 5th, just as I had dreamed.

There are no words to describe what becoming a mother did for me. Oh how in love I was with this little being! Even when he was sound asleep I never wanted to put him down; I just wanted to stare into his perfect, beautiful face and make sure he was still breathing and safe. Having him in my arms, close to my heart, was like holding a thousand Christmases of gifts. I already felt that he would be my best friend and so I whispered to him my every thought and emotion as if he already could understand me, and I planned all the things I would do for him...and not do. I'm certain that every mother swears to do a better job than their mother did, and so we make our silent vows. Though they are deeply heartfelt, genuine and well-intended, at some point we fail. There is no such thing as the perfect mother; we all just do the best we can according to what we have been equipped with.

My newborn son, in a sense, was a savior to me; whatever cruelties I had been willing to endure with Terry, I was NOT willing to have my son suffer, and so that gave me the strength to never again enter into a relationship with Terry. We continued to live with Sylvia for a few months, but she lost her job and I was receiving a meager sum from welfare, so we could not keep up the apartment. My mother had said goodbye to Pete, again, swearing this time it was permanent, so back I went to live with her and my little sister who had finally been able to leave my father's home and move in as well.

As my little wonder grew, it was evident that he was highly intelligent as well as adorable. I now and forever-more had a phenomenal reason for living. My mother and sister both were completely enamored with him, and so he became the little prince with three queen mothers to dote on him. We often took long walks around the neighbor-hood and on one such walk we passed by a little white and blue church with a smiling little white haired man out front who waved at us. My mother's apartment was only 2 blocks away. I, out of shame, had stopped going to the previous church ever since I found out I was pregnant. Now, this church seemed to be drawing me. I did not attend right away, but often a group of people from the church would come in and eat at a nearby deli where I was now employed, and on several occasions had invited me to come. Finally, I did. Austin was two.

Months later, I was invited to come and live with a family from the church who thought it would be a good idea for Austin to have a father figure in his life. There were a few other people from broken homes or broken lives living there as well. I lived there about a year before meeting my husband. Charlie would always talk to me after church, and though I was not attracted to him at first, his heart and soul of gold shone through his eyes and, eventually, he won me over.

We walked down the aisle to become Mr. and Mrs. Forman on August 9th, 1985; Austin was 3 ½ . I had prayed not only for a husband that would truly love me but one that would be a good father to my son as well. God answered that prayer. At birth, I had given Austin Terry's last name since he was his biological father, but within a few months after our wedding, Charlie started the process to legally adopt him. Paperwork finished, sitting in court waiting for the final step of the adoption, Terry showed up. He had received a summons informing him of Charlie's intent to adopt, but he had not responded to me or our lawyer, so we were all shocked to see him there trying to contest it. After some questioning, it was evident to the judge that Terry had made little effort to be part of Austin's life, and never provided for him, so his parental rights were stripped and Austin became a Forman.

By the time of that court date, I had already added to our family by giving birth to our daughter Hannah. So in love once again, as I had been with Austin. When Charlie would go off to work and Austin to Kindergarten, I would crawl back in bed with Hannah to snuggle and marvel for a while, and I would sing a little song my heart had made up from this overflowing love I felt. It went like this: "Hannah Gracie, Hannah Gracie, little girl with the pretty facie, Hannah, Hannah, I love you." My son had made me a mother and given me a reason to live and a joy in my heart that I had never known; now, Hannah Grace, my little girl, introduced me to the new wonders of having a daughter. Little did I know in naming her that how true it would be of her character as she grew...full of grace; give you the shirt off her back kind of girl. My heart and life were full, and I tried to be the perfect mother. Silent prayers and spoken vows promised to never let anything harm them or cause them pain, especially not the things that had damaged me.

The pendulum now swayed full swing in the other direction. As far as I had swung into rebellious ways, I had now swung to the other end of extremes, trying desperately to do all things perfect and steer clear of any error. The perfect wife, the perfect mother, the perfect Christian and upstanding citizen. My previous ways had ruined my life, in fact, almost ended it, so of course I wanted to be as far removed as possible from that path and behavior.

Within the next five years, I gave birth to two more children: Samuel...how was it possible to be so equally in love with another son? Then came Madelon, the answer to Hannah's prayers and mine as she completed our family with a wonderful balance of two boys and two girls. Four wonderful children...redeeming/reclaiming the four abortions?

I never knew such happiness existed. I was so in love with all four of these perfect little beings; they became my whole world. Open face peanut butter sandwiches with banana slices for eyes and raisins for the pupils and also to form a smile, handmade fabric painted pillow cases and t-shirts with their favorite designs and characters, heart shaped meals on Valentine's Day, silly songs, playing at the park, long hearty laughter, reading books, bubble baths, round-the-clock hugs and kissing boo-boos, bedtime prayers, finding as many ways as possible to lavish love on these little ones; such were my days now. Quite a contrast to my former life.

A Little Girl's Dreams

I look upon my little girl's face
Such sweetness in her eyes
I think of another time and place
And ponder how time flies

Twas yesterday that once was mine
With wonder in my heart
Today she takes my place in line
In life to do her part

In her smile the joy of childhood dreams
Her eyes show the hope she holds
I pray that all is as it seems
As each dream soon unfolds

Will she be all I never could?
Do all I never did?
Grasping all that's pleasant and good
That deep in my heart I hid

I will rejoice with you little girl
Not mourn for what has been
For all life's joys as they unfurl
Through you are mine again

Little Boys

A newborn baby boy is sweet
But soon he'll grow and have muddy feet
And track it all across your rug
All because he wanted to give you a hug

He's no trouble now, though he sometimes cries
And you look at him with loving sighs
But will you think he's just as swell
When his boyish antics make you want to yell?

Each year will bring ten tons of dirt
He'll fall down often and cry cause he's hurt
He'll drive you crazy at the mall
Torture his sister but that's not all

He's sure to break at least a few dishes
Bring bugs in the house against your wishes
But just when you think you can't take anymore
You'll find him fast asleep on the floor

You'll brush back the hair from his angelic face
In your heart once again he's found a place
Memories of dirt and trouble…there are none
As you kiss his brow and thank God for your son

The more attention I gave my children, the less my husband received. It was not intentional; I was not even aware of it. Though I still loved him deeply, it's as if something inside of me took control and I was determined to not repeat what I felt my mother had done…choosing Pete over her children. I would not let a man cause me to do the same. Obviously, this began to affect our marriage. Feeling neglected, my husband thrust himself more into work. He had become a real estate appraiser, eventually starting his own business. This took a lot of time and energy and often he had already left the house in the morning before the children were awake to get ready for school. Again, in the evening, many times the children were in bed before he returned. We lived in two separate, very different worlds, and each of us had little understanding or patience for the other. We still had a deep and bonding love for one another, but it was now subterranean; buried beneath the bruised egos, harsh words and bleeding hearts of mixed emotions. Why couldn't I see that he was just lashing out because he was longing for my love and attention, and that part of the reason for his concentrated work schedule was to provide for those he loved? Why couldn't he see how important the children were and that they are only small for such a short time? Too many sweet, cherished moments were slipping between his fingers as I alone witnessed the wonder of their precious and fleeting childhood. Only God could intervene at this point to enlighten our clouded and stubborn minds…and he did. As always in my life, since that first time that I had opened my heart to him, dying in the back seat of that car at the swap meet, he has always been faithful to rescue me.

At least we were all together as a family on the weekends, and we were very involved in our church. My husband's desire had always been to be a pastor, and an opportunity came about to take over a small church in Little Rock… California, not Arkansas, like most think when I mention the name. It is desert area on the outskirts of Palmdale. We excitedly packed up our belongings and babies and headed to the desert to begin our new adventure. The rescue was that even though my husband continued his real estate appraisal business, his focus was now redirected, family and God taking center stage, and it benefited us all.

There were only a handful of people in the church, but we were hopeful and joyful as we reached out to the surrounding neighborhoods inviting them to church. Our children were delighted to participate and help in the services wherever and whenever they could. My husband, in between pastoring the church, was occasionally commuting about an hour and a half to L.A. attempting to continue his appraisal business. Whenever he could though, he worked from home. I home schooled the children since we could not find a good school close by. We were all quite content... for a time. Family life was great, but after two years with little growth in the church and Charlie's appraisal business experiencing great difficulties, the decision was made to let the church go and move back to L.A. We had gone out with joy and high hopes, but returned with a faith as dry as the desert itself, and nothing but a handful of dust. Or did we? We went out with the intentions of building a church, but maybe it was our family that had been rebuilt and strengthened.

There is always a greater design than what meets the eye. An ulterior plan far greater than our own is always being constructed. As life throws us curve balls, and we reach and stretch to try to swing at them, our strength and character are being built. Little Rock had been our training ground. Though Charlie did still work, his, and our main focus had been one and the same…the church. It brought a unity and a strength to our family that had not been there before. Though the church had not been a success, and we felt a little defeated, we were glad to be back among those we knew and loved in a busy church.

Our church has a school and I was offered a job teaching there. My youngest, Madelon, was three at the time, and I was allowed to bring her to the school while I taught. Hannah was almost 9 and was in my class. My sons, Austin and Sam, also attended the school. For the next five years, I continued to teach. My days were full of planning lessons and correcting work as well as raising my children. Dinners, homework, school events, church events; I even wrote a musical during this time. My husband built his real estate appraisal business back up and we all had full schedules. Life was hectic, but we were content once again. The years when my children were young were my happiest by far. Through grueling days at work, arguments with my husband, or whatever other hardships came in life; my children were a constant source of joy for me. I had never felt love like this before; neither given nor received.

Love's Anchor

My children are an anchor
That tethers me to Earth
The only worldly possession
That I've cherished since their birth

If not for them I think this world
Could never make me stay
I'd beg to join my Jesus
Where all tears have passed away

Although I pine for Heaven
I know there's work to do
And four little perfect faces beam
To say they need me too

So until my time for Heaven comes
I'll give my heart to Earth
Ever thankful for my anchor
Who'll never know their worth

Nevertheless, there was still another constant in my life, an undercurrent of depression and fear caused by the damage done in my childhood. Always with me was the feeling that I did not really belong in this world; that I was less than others, a mistake and a stupid piece of #@%*, unworthy and undeserving of true happiness, so I lived with the fear of it all being taken away from me. Every time a problem arose or a disappointment came, panic would strike and I was sure, like Chicken Little, that the whole sky was falling. This affected my relationship with my husband and with God. It was difficult and even a bit frightening to trust my husband; I never doubted his faithfulness to me, but to trust him with decisions for our family or even the care of the children was distressing. Since I thought of God as a father figure, and I did not have any point of reference for what a good, loving father was, when things went wrong I quickly felt unloved and unworthy. Though well masked most days, there was always an interior battle. Some days I triumphed and felt on top of the world, some days I lost and felt the world was on top of me. I thought I had found the key to freedom— to a certain degree, I did. I had walked out free from drugs and my past, however; I still, in a sense, felt locked in. One door had opened, like a prison cell door, but it was as if I was still wandering down a long corridor through life with yet another door still a long way off in front of me. I was still searching for the key to that last door and ultimate freedom on the outside. Because I felt out of control on the inside, I tried to control everything on the outside. I was overprotective of my children, forever fearful that something would happen to them. My weight constantly fluctuated; when life felt like a stream of unsolvable problems to me I would either eat everything I desired as a comfort, or practically starve myself to be thin and in my mind more worthy; either way, the reason was the same... my body was the only thing I had complete control over when life felt out of control.

After five years of teaching, life had become so routine, stressful, and burdensome that I felt suffocated. I remember standing on the playground of the school at recess time, tears welling up in my eyes, thinking that if this is what the rest of my life is to be...why live? I could not continue; I needed a break and a change. I finished out the school year but decided to homeschool my children the following year to change things up and relieve some of the pressure and stress. We all have hopes and dreams, but life interrupts and takes us on a detour. Though there is pain along the path, there are also pleasant surprises. After a year of homeschooling, one of those pleasant surprises came and it changed all of our lives forever.

A couple had been attending our church for some time; the husband was Dutch, but the wife was French. One day at a church function, I saw her across the yard and that same small inner voice inside me spoke and said, "I want you to pick up your French again." I approached her and asked if she had ever considered giving French lessons. She grinned and said, " I can't believe this, I was just talking to the pastor about how much I love this church and wished that there was someone who could be sent to start a church like it in France." I hardly knew her and had never really had a conversation with her before, so I had no idea that they were planning to move back to France. The pastor told her to just pray and God would provide someone. I found out later that actually he had thought perhaps they would start a church there. God had other plans. She and I immediately settled on Tuesday nights for French lessons and it was opened to others to attend as well. A handful of us had been meeting for a month or two when she announced that she would be gone for a couple of weeks visiting her family in France. I joked with her to take me in her suitcase, my lifelong dream having been to see France before I die. She, not joking, said that if I could buy my plane ticket I could come along on the trip and stay at her parent's home with her in Versailles. That eliminates a lot of expense, not having to pay for a hotel. During these months of rekindling my passion for French, there was another kindling being ignited in my heart. In our fellowship of churches, where there are multiple churches worldwide, I knew there was no church, as yet, in France. Often, returning home on Tuesday evenings, I would mention this to my husband. My dream was France; his was still to be a pastor, even after the failure of Little Rock. I would try to incite him to desire to start a church in France, but my efforts were unproductive. Now, I was willing to settle for this trip. He agreed to let me go. Though this couple stayed for a few weeks, I was only able to be away for 8 days, due to responsibilities. I marveled at every sight, smell and sensation as I walked through the streets of the cities of Versailles and Paris. I visited the chateau in Versailles and was awestruck to be walking on the same tile floors where all the kings of France had walked. It truly was a dream come true and I was grateful. I had printed out some pamphlets with a message in French telling the people that God loved them and passed out a few here and there as my thank you to God for the gift of this trip. I kept a journal during my eight days, not wanting to ever forget a minute of it. On the last day there, I wrote in it a short prayer. It went something like this: "God, thank you for this trip and a dream come true. I feel such a love for the French people and really believe we are supposed to come start a church here. If this is not from you, I give you permission to remove it from my heart, and I will just be thankful for and treasure this trip. But, if this IS what we are supposed to do, speak to my husband and put it in his heart." I returned thinking surely it would be me that would have it taken out of my heart, nevertheless, I was thankful that I had seen France before I died. I was shocked to learn that my husband had an experience while I was gone and believed that we were in fact supposed to start a church there. He spoke to our pastor and things were put in motion to move towards that goal.

With almost everything in place for this huge transition in our life, the one thing holding me back was my oldest son, Austin, 19 at the time. He had moved out and was not living life in the manner we had raised him to, therefore; he was not interested in coming with us to start a church. This shattered my heart. I told him that if he wanted us to stay, I would. He assured me though that we should go, saying that just because he didn't want to go do something for God didn't mean that we shouldn't. We continued to move ahead with our plans, yet, not without many tears shed on my part at the thought of leaving my first born behind. At 19, Austin was an adult, but my other children were still young enough that there was no question about whether they would come with us. Hannah was 15, Sam 12, and Madelon 8 ½ .

We tried to prepare and equip them by listening to a tape series of French lessons. I already knew the foundation of the grammar and the basics of vocabulary from high school days, but my husband had taken Spanish in school so he learned along with the children. We gave away most of what we owned as far as furniture and other belongings, keeping only our clothes, some books, guitars, and a few items of memorabilia. Baby books and photo albums were left behind in storage. With the house emptied and suitcases packed, we were finally ready to embark on the adventure of a lifetime.

Having turned in the keys to our house, we spent our last night in America at my mother's apartment. We were to be at the airport by 1:30 p.m. the following day. I awoke to the panicked voice of my mother asking me where Hannah was. It was around 7 a.m., my night owl of a girl would never have been up that early; we realized she must have snuck out in the middle of the night. At 15, she was not thrilled to leave her friends behind and move to another country. We thought we had worked through it, but apparently at the last minute, she and a friend had schemed a plan for her to run away.

I frantically started calling all her friends to see if she was there; they all said she was not. We were supposed to be at the airport in a matter of hours to move to another country, and I could not find my daughter. My husband decided to drive around looking for her. I called the friend she had been spending most of her time with, again, asking her if she had shown up there and begging her to call me if she heard from her. I was crying and pleading, having a gut feeling that she at least knew something...suddenly I heard the girl's brother in the background screaming at her saying, "Just tell her !" He then grabbed the phone and told me that Hannah WAS in fact there. My husband had returned from circling around in his car; without even answering this boy on the phone I looked at my husband and silently formed the words with my lips, "she's there" and quickly motioned to him to go while I tried to keep them on the phone. He was able to get there and retrieve our daughter with just enough time for us to all get to the airport on time. To say the least, this was not the best of beginnings as we set out on this great adventure.

Our first few weeks in France were full of new discoveries and adjusting to the time difference. Charlie and I were full of wonder, anticipation and hope; Hannah was still sullen over leaving her country and comrades. Sam and Madelon were young and content to tag along on the adventure.

Our first month there was quite eventful. We quickly discovered the pros and cons of their medical system. Hannah came down with tonsillitis which turned into an abscess. At first, I was not aware of the severity because, unbeknownst to me, our thermometer was broken and she did not appear to have a high fever. However, after days of her not even being able to swallow water or move from her bed, I was more than concerned. I did not yet know of any doctors or hospitals or even where to call for this information. It was evening, and it was the weekend. The French friend from our church in L.A. had moved back to France, so I called her. They were in fact to be part of helping us build the church there, but at the moment, they were on vacation visiting family in another town. We had no car as yet. I was able to reach her and she told me that in France they still do house calls for a small additional fee. She gave me a number to call and told me to give my address and they would send a doctor from the area. She instructed me to be sure and say it was "grave"… "serious". I dialed the number and explained my daughter's condition to the voice on the other end of the phone. She responded with what I thought was the word "grave," so I responded, "Oui, c'est grave/ yes, it's serious." Confusingly though, she then said they could not send a doctor. I did not understand and repeated that it was "grave!" She repeated, I thought, "grave", but again said she could not send a doctor; there were none available. That much I understood. Flustered and desperate, I called my friend once again and asked her to call for me. She did. When she called me back to explain, she tried not to chuckle because of the gravity of the situation, but informed me that what I mistakenly took the woman to be saying as "grave" was actually "grève" which in French means strike…the doctors were on strike! The good news was that she searched and was able to find a doctor willing to come to the apartment and Hannah received the medical attention and medicine needed just in time. According to the doctor, the abscess was serious and one more day could have led to the infection spreading throughout her body. Shortly after that, our next medical emergency was Sam. He and Madelon were playing around and she pushed him; he stumbled backward into the bathroom, his head hitting a glass shelf, which shattered and cut his head. It was a pretty deep gash and he needed stitches. My husband called our friends this time. They were now back in town, and the two husbands drove Sam to the hospital. They did not numb his head before stitching it; glad I wasn't there. The positive in all of it was that doctors and medicine are inexpensive in France.

The last event in our eventful first month was a phone call I received. Terry, Austin's biological father, had died. It was Austin himself who called me with the news. During his turbulent teenage years, Austin, bucking Charlie's discipline, was convinced that life would be different and better if only he had his biological father. Though I had warned him what Terry was like, he was still determined. Long story short, I found him for him. Austin went to live with him for a few months, but swiftly realized his error and that he had been under a delusion. He called one day wanting to speak to Charlie. When Charlie asked him how things were going with his dad...Austin responded, "He may be my father, but he is not my dad; YOU are my dad." Grateful tears were shed at this realization. This all took place before we left for France and is why Austin was the one contacted by Terry's mother to announce his death. I was greatly saddened by the news because Terry had never changed his partying ways and died from damage to his liver due to alcohol. Though I had once walked down that same road in life, I chose to change paths and in so doing chose life; someone I once cared for never saw the danger sign, never changed direction, and inadvertently chose death, and it deeply grieved me.

On the positive side of things, Hannah not only recovered from her illness, but also from her sullen state. One day, a young girl knocked on our door selling something for her school. She was around Hannah's age.

Though Hannah knew little French and the girl knew little English, Hannah grabbed her French/English dictionary and they somehow found a way to communicate. The girl, whose name is Jennifer, lived in our building and had two sisters. Not only did a friendship start, but so did our church. We found out that the mother of these three girls had died a few years back, and Jennifer had been a mother to her two younger sisters since the age of twelve. The father worked a lot but also drank a lot to cover his pain, thus; he was not really doing much parenting other than providing an apartment. Jennifer bought the groceries and cooked, did laundry and whatever else was necessary for the care of the home and the girls. Madelon became friends with the two younger sisters: Axelle and Cindy, who were only a year apart. We did not, as of yet, have a building for our church so we gathered for services in the living room of our apartment. The three sisters were our first members and the first of many sorrowful souls to cross our path during our years in France. They were so in need of love and attention and I became a mother figure to them. They looked to my husband as well for guidance. My children provided the fun; they were ever intrigued by this American family.

A couple more people were added to the little church in our living room, however, we had landed in Cassis as a starting point. It was a quaint and breathtakingly beautiful coastal village and we were happy to soak in its charms during our stay. The port was lined on one side by turquoise waters and small boats, the other side lined with restaurants and shops. Above it all stood hills and cliffs of limestone. We made lasting friendships in the town and learned so much about the country and customs. Our friends had found this apartment for us and we were grateful to have a home to come to arriving in France, but our final destination had always been Marseille, the second largest city in France. A much better place to build a church. We spent fifteen months in Cassis getting grounded, but also it took that long to obtain an apartment in Marseille. The bureaucracy was complicated. Our apartment in Cassis was what they call a "seasonal", meaning a vacation home. This meant, in our case, that it was owned by a couple that lived in Paris, but who kept this apartment as well as their summer vacation home. All their belongings were still in it. Short term vacation rentals were not a problem. Finding a permanent apartment of our own was difficult due to the fact that not only were we foreigners, but we did not have a normal job there that could provide pay stubs for proof of income. We needed to acquire a letter from our pastor as well as bank statements from the church, etc. This was an unprecedented case for them and many rental agencies turned us down for fear of getting stuck in a messy affair. There are different laws in France, and if we were granted an apartment and couldn't pay afterward, the red tape to evict us could take over a year. Nobody wanted to take that risk. We continued to search but were obligated to move three times in Cassis from seasonal to seasonal as we waited. Out of options with the arrival of summer, we moved into the back house of our friends. This was short lived, as there was a falling-out between us. It is not worth repeating the details but suffices to say that they had their own agenda and were not really with us in this venture of starting a church. Finally, mercifully, just in time, we found an apartment in Marseille willing to take a chance on us.

What a relief and a joy to have our own apartment at last to call home, even if we didn't have furniture yet! Fifteen months of basically living out of our suitcases since the seasonal was not only furnished, but the people even had their clothes hanging in the closets! Finally, I could empty my suitcase. Our church back home sent us money to furnish the apartment. I realized the effect all those months had on us all when Madelon, then nine and a half, sat mesmerized and entertained planted in front of our newly acquired washing machine during the entire wash cycle. Also, no one complained as we slowly added to the furnishings of our home, having no real beds yet, only mattresses on the floor. The things we take for granted become a great luxury when one has not had the simple amenities of one's own home.

We had a car now and Cassis was just over the hill, so we saw the girls often. Whenever possible, we drove to Cassis to pick them up for church. We still did not have a building since we had just moved to Marseille, and renting a building for the purpose of a church brought a whole other slew of red tape bureaucracy, so we continued to meet in our living room. Charlie and I enrolled in a local university course for a semester to improve our French and in doing so he made friends with a group of Chinese students who were also there for their French. This was the beginning of our church in Marseille, the French girls and the Chinese students. Next, Hannah met some Nigerians at a bus stop who also became part of the church. Finally, we were able to obtain a building and the church grew. Marseille is an international melting pot and I loved having our little church of mixed nations. It is also a city of transients though with people from all over the world passing through; some visiting, others come from poor countries hoping to find work. We had our small core group of people faithful to come, but so many others that came for just a while on their way passing through from places like Romania, Germany, Russia, other African countries and just about everywhere in Europe. We even had a gypsy man who, much to our surprise, came faithfully for a month. Though we had experienced struggles and opposition the first few years, we were now established and living out the dream. Not that life WAS a dream or carefree; we had little money, and trying to reach the hearts of the French people with the love of God proved to be challenging. If you trace the history of France it is evident why they would be leery. Throughout the ages, they were controlled and manipulated by either the government or the Catholic church, and so for many, their slogan became, "Ni Dieu ni maitre" which means: neither God nor master. They pride themselves now on their independence and freedom to be and do as they wish. It was difficult for them to understand that we, being Christians, or what they refer to as protestants, were unlike Catholics (this is no slam on Catholics; I am talking about centuries old behavior) and that we were interested in helping them and not controlling them. They only understood this with relationship and time…a lot of time. Five years into this mission we still had a mere handful of people attending the church on a regular basis. Our hearts were full though, full of love for the people and the country, still full of hope for the future, and full of joy to be living out what we felt was our calling and purpose. France was still a dream for me, despite the hardships.

The Missionary

"Going home", the missionary smiles
As his thoughts wander across the miles
Memories of places and people so dear
Wash back anew through a flood of tears

"Ah", he thinks, "Won't it be grand?"
After so long a stranger on foreign land
To be once again on familiar soil
To cease for a moment from all his toil

He's greeted warmly when he arrives
Once again sharing in many lives
Though he's joyful, there's a truth that can't be denied
He's STILL the stranger looking in from outside

Blurred Lines

Though familiar and forever engraved in his heart
There's a distance, for he, is no longer a part
He knows things will never again be the same
And that, for a time, home has changed its name

His heart starts to long for things far away
People and places now a part of everyday
For they have gained their place as well
And the missionary's heart begins to swell

And so he lives each day, each year
With thoughts of home that bring a tear
Yet, each day, also comforted knowing
He's fulfilling destiny with seeds he is sowing

He's a pilgrim and never really at home
Destined, for a time, two countries to roam
But though he's a stranger at home and abroad
He's well known and at home in the presence of God

Even in the entire eight years in total that we spent there, the thrill of certain daily pleasures of living there never dulled. Walking outside of my front door and hearing people speaking French all around me... the most beautiful language in the world, the exquisite architecture of their buildings and statues, a warm baguette fresh from the bakery with any one of the four-hundred cheeses they make, their coffee and chocolate, their humorous phrases, mannerisms and gestures, the lavender fields or red poppies that cover the land, and many other intricacies that lay between the many lovely limestone hills and the placid beaches. My love for this country and its people was so deep that speaking to them about a God who also loved them deeply came so naturally. Everywhere I went, this was the natural outflow from my heart to my mouth. The woman at the bakery, a stranger on the bus, the owner of the fruit and vegetable stand at the end of our street, our neighbors, the fellow dog walkers in the park behind our building, and so on.

The Funny thing is, even though the French are hesitant to trust in God, they love to debate. I walked our dog Bijou daily in the little park behind our building and had frequent conversations with a few men who also brought their dogs daily. Often my conversations would be with a man from our same building named Gerard, sometimes with a man named Guy, occasionally another man whose name I can not remember would come join the conversation as well. On one particular day, all three of them were there. I entered the park and also entered the conversation, which soon turned into a theological debate. I wish I had a video recording of it all. What a sight that must have been, three French men of which one was an atheist, one a Deist, the other an animist—the belief that even plants and animals have souls and we are all gods, in a sense, as part of the universe, and then there was me, the little American, Christian woman. The debate became pretty heated and I was sure none of them would want to speak to me again. To my shock, the next time I ventured into the park, sheepishly, at seeing all three of them there again, they all greeted me as if I was their best friend! Many days of conversation and friendship ensued, especially with Gerard. I discovered his life story and why he became an atheist.

He was a child during the holocaust and his father was Jewish; his mother was Catholic. Since they lived in the south of France, they had only heard of what was going on with the Germans in the northern parts of France in the beginning stages of the Holocaust and didn't quite believe all of it or understand the severity. Gerard's father took a job in the North and boarded a train, against the warnings of many. He was intercepted by German soldiers and died in the camps. Because Gerard was half Jewish, they were looking for him as well, even though he was only about two years old at the time; his name was on a list. His mother, being Catholic, was not in danger but sent Gerard to live with relatives hidden in the hills. He was able to return to his mother after a couple of years when the war ended, but he grew up seeing the devastation all this caused his mother. She never remarried, and since she had never held a job prior to marrying Gerard's father, she struggled her whole life with odd side jobs to clothe and feed her son. His mother's sorrow and suffering along with the slaughter of a father he would never know provided the seeds from which his atheism grew. As he told me the story, he said, "I will never forgive." I gave him a copy of Corrie ten Boom's *The Hiding Place*. Gerard was an odd case to me though. He was not like others I had met who held on to anger and chose to close themselves off from people; he was extremely friendly, smiled easily, and often had a joke. Many times someone would stroll through the park with their dog and he would point them out to me and tell me about their life. He seemed to genuinely love people and put them at ease. I always enjoyed our talks in the park.

Gerard was not the only mystery on my list of sorrowful souls. There is Sophie. Sophie was born on the miniscule island of Réunion which is located in the Indian Ocean. It is a tiny dot to the east of Madagascar, which does not even appear on some maps. Her mother was a drug addict who had a string of dysfunctional relationships. Sophie was the product of one of those relationships, and she also had a half sister who was the issue of a different relationship. Both were placed in an orphanage at a tender age; their mother was unable and/or unwilling to care for them. She did, however, visit them sporadically. It is unfathomable to me the treatment that Sophie endured at the hand of her own mother. She would come offering hugs and a gift for her sister, but nothing for Sophie. Sophie attributes this to the fact that she was dark skinned, dark eyed and frizzy-haired, while her sister was blond haired, blue eyed and light skinned. Their father was a dark-skinned islander; the mother white. Shocking that any mother could be prejudiced against her own child isn't it? The visits then ceased and the two sisters were placed in separate foster homes. For Sophie, it turned into a string of foster homes…never receiving love or affection from any of them. At 17 she decided to set out on her own. She found a menial job and a place to stay and was content to at least be free. She was lonely though, still longing to be loved, and quickly fell prey to the first man that paid attention to her. He turned out to be unfaithful as well as abusive... yet another form of rejection to crush Sophie's already badly bruised heart. Eventually the relationship ended but she soon met and married another man with whom she had a son. He was not much different than the first man. He came home only when he felt like it and barely provided for her and their son; Sophie had to work hard to make ends meet. Finally, he left as well. The cycle repeated itself one more time with yet another man, which produced another son. By the time I met Sophie she had three past abusive relationships, two sons and was missing her two front teeth. A man from our church, one of the Nigerians, met her first and brought her to church. She experienced there, for the first time, a true and pure love, the love of God. In spite of all the heartbreaking violations in her life, she became so full of joy that members of the church took to calling her Sister Joy. She did not hold any grudge or bitterness but forgave all who had hurt her. Though she had little money and worked hard for the little she had, she was extremely generous. She also gave of her time, and at church functions would bring the best homemade fried chicken I have ever tasted. She and the man who brought her to church were married and my heart burst with joy as well at the thought of her finally finding a decent, loving man after all the abuse she had suffered. Sadly, the marriage only lasted about seven years. In her husband's African culture having a child, particularly a son to carry on the family name, is of utmost importance. For him, it was even more important since he was the only male in his family. Sophie was in her forties by now and though she took fertility treatments, tried in vitro and whatever else was available to try to give him a child, she remained barren. Occasionally, her husband would travel back to Nigeria to visit family and on one such visit he took a young wife who instantly became pregnant, and Sophie was abandoned once again.

I was horrified and nauseated by the news of it and could not imagine what this might do to someone who had already suffered so much devastation in her life. She was deeply grieved by it, of course, but resiliently continued not only to come to church services but to help and show love to others. This was proof that despite her husband's betrayal, she would not be swayed from the one true love she HAD found...God's love. She is a hero to me. Many would have blamed God; in fact, many would have never made it through half of what Sophie had endured in life without remaining permanently scarred and bitter. Sophie, without a doubt, slew the dragon.

There were many others we encountered, wounded, woeful, wandering. Reaching out to help and love them brought a certain healing to my own soul. Unfortunately, my own troubles and woes were far from over.

Because of all I had suffered in my youth, I did everything in my power to protect my children from a similar fate and had warned them of the evils of this world, the temptations, and the consequences. Despite all this, every human must choose their own path and learn their own lessons as they stumble over the pebbles and rocks strewn along that path. Over time, each one of my children would shatter my heart with choices they made.

The Prodigal

She tried the world on for size
But soon she tired of its lies
And wearied of wearing its false disguise

Such is the way with glittering sin
It catches the eye and drags you in
But soon what seemed gold turns to tin

An empty cup made of tin
An empty heart battered within
And haunting memories of where you've been

Your shoulders weren't made for such a load
Nor your feet made to walk such a rocky road
But to stroll golden streets in a heavenly abode

Change the direction of your path
Flee the world and its coming wrath
Be cleansed of your sin and its aftermath

Lift your eyes to the Heavens above
Give your life to the God of love
For He knows just what your dreams are made of

He wants to make your life complete
Bring victory where you've had defeat
So fall weary child at your Savior's feet

Austin had already done so, walking away from everything he was taught growing up in the church and in our home. He got into drugs, and as I can personally attest to, substances cause you to do things that would never naturally enter into your mind to do. You become another person. Many mornings were spent with uncontrollable sobs coming from the depths of my gut because I awoke to find he had not come home and not only did I not know where he was, but because of his lifestyle I did not know if he was even alive.

The details are not mine to tell; it is my son's story to tell someday, but I can tell you that his actions brought sorrow and shame to the whole family. He was forgiven and relationship was restored, but my heart still ached for him over the broken dreams left in the dust as he deviated down a dead end.

Now, here in France, it was Hannah who was next to twist the knife already lodged into my heart. She had a couple of years of rebelling against all we had taught her as well, questioning and experimenting, and along the way met a man nine years her senior, from Egypt, who had been raised a Muslim. Though they had only known each other a short time, they wanted to marry. Knowing nothing about Sameh, we were against the marriage on principle alone. He was too old for her and came from a culture that is unfavorable towards women and has opposing religious beliefs. This was not the prince I had dreamed of for my little princess and I was afraid. The dreams and hopes I had for all my children were one by one being shattered, first with Austin, now with Hannah. Each new blow dug the dagger a bit deeper into my soul and further dimmed the vision of my eyes from seeing a hopeful future for any of us.

Sameh knew of my concerns and invited me to have lunch with them one day. I accepted, fully intending to go there and set them both straight and state my reasons for my disapproval, however; not long into the meal a peace came over me and that same small, inner voice was telling me that it would be alright. I learned that he had left Egypt because he was not in agreement with some of the ways of the culture. He traveled to Europe on a quest to find truth. He believed in God but was searching for answers and instinctively knew they were not to be found in his own country. This comforted me, along with the fact that there was just something in his eyes that reassured me that his heart and his intentions could be trusted. My grandmother always told me that the eyes are the window to the soul and it has proved true. The more I got to know Sameh, the more my soul was at rest that God would work it all out for good, and I not only accepted their relationship but grew to love him. However, my husband had no peace at all about it. At first, he stated to me that he would not attend the wedding. I thank God for wise counsel from a friend of his who told us two true stories with similar situations where opposite decisions were made with two frighteningly different outcomes. We heeded the warning that if we rejected Sameh, and refused to go to the wedding, we would lose our daughter in the process. It was clear that though we may not have been in agreement with the marriage, we needed to love and support our daughter. In so doing we would have relationship and influence with both Hannah and Sameh. Thankfully, this did turn out to be the case, but it has not always been an easy road. They have had their struggles and our hearts ached along with hers as God slowly but faithfully smoothed out the bumps in the road. Again, it is Hannah's story to tell the details; I will not betray her.

After one year of marriage, Hannah and Sameh decided to move back to America. It seemed to be the best choice for their future; there were more job opportunities and other advantages there to facilitate building a family. Though I was happy for them, my heart was greatly wounded by the departure of my daughter/confidante/best friend. Our last few years in France I was never quite the same. I even wrote a poem during that time about how the whole world seemed to have turned to a dismal gray after Hannah left. I fought depression, yet, one positive result was that my relationship with my youngest daughter, Madelon, grew closer. This was my saving grace, along with the fact that I found joy in helping those more wounded than myself, like Sophie and others.

One year later my son Sam decided to move back to America. He was now 18 and wanted to finish his last year of high school with friends. A family from our church in Santa Monica offered Sam the opportunity to come live with them. I strongly protested; I already had been separated from two of my children, Austin, and Hannah, now I was expected to live without yet another of my four most precious treasures? Fireworks were going off in my head; thoughts shooting here and there as to why this was not an acceptable decision. My heart now completely pierced through by the knife already lodged and twisted there. My husband thought it would be beneficial to Sam and so, I, being the minority, lost the battle. It was October, we were in Santa Monica, having returned for our church's annual pastors' conference, and we now boarded the plane to return to France without my third child. With a heavy heart, I tried my best to continue to serve the people in our church, carrying out my normal functions, though feeling wounded and handicapped. December came and it was difficult to be cheery or even want to decorate. Christmases were usually quite the family event in our home, baking cookies, laughing, watching Christmas movies, picking out the tree and decorating it together. Now, I had only one child left, and our home was eerily quiet. Thank God for that one child, Madelon. She kept asking when we were going to get the Christmas stuff out and decorate; seeing that I just didn't have the heart, she took it upon herself and surprised me one day, actually doing a much better job of it than I would have. She tried to usher in some holiday cheer and lighten my heart, but when Christmas morning came Charlie had the flu. He dragged himself out of bed to see Madelon open her two small gifts, all we could afford, and then he went back to bed. Madelon and I sat side by side on the couch, peering around the empty, silent apartment, both of us depressed now. No laughter, no other children, no piles of wrapping paper to clean up as we prepare for breakfast like usual, no other smiling family faces to wish a Merry Christmas to or to join us in any kind of celebration of the day; no amount of Christmas music could cheer our hearts now. It was only eleven o'clock in the morning, but we were sorely ready for the day to be over. I think I remained in a funk until February.

I tried to carry on but longed to go home to America. My oldest son had a second son by now, so with his family, Hannah, and now Sam, I had more family in America than here in France and it weighed on me daily. I began asking my husband if we could return. Actually, begging him. I also voiced my desire to our pastor. The two of them believed that it was not time for us to return yet. I struggled for two more years. Sometimes I had a good attitude about it, sometimes I did not. The next Christmas that came around I tried not to think of my own lack of family but focus on the many members of our church who were also far from family. I actually found great joy in decorating the church and baking for them as I would have for my own family. After all, the reason we came here in the first place was to bring hope to the hurting. Sometimes though I was angry with my husband, feeling like he was so callous and oblivious to the pain in my heart over my children. He either couldn't see or didn't care that I had been crippled by Hannah and Sam leaving. He seemed to be so self- involved with the work of the church that I was either invisible or an annoying roadblock to his destination. My life, in my eyes, did not seem to matter to him. I became bitter and our marriage suffered like never before. We could not be in the same room for five minutes without arguing and we grew so cold towards each other that I did not think there was any hope for us to love one another again. Though our love had died, I would not dare bury it by divorce; not only did we both believe divorce was wrong but we both knew the devastation it causes families. Being a product of divorce myself, I knew the repercussions it would have on my children's' lives, and so I would not even entertain the thought. This being the case, my only option was to stay in a relationship that seemed to be a mere business partnership, and a poor one at that. Living the rest of my life without love was the most desperately hopeless thought I had ever had, but I couldn't envision our love resurrecting. Could the God who had rescued me so many times before do it again? I had to believe so and hope, not only for my sake but for the sake of the example it would be for my children, especially my daughters.

Our relationship started to improve as we forgave each other's shortcomings; there was now a glimmer of hope. We traveled together to another city in France, Tours, to help out another fellow church with an event they were having. From there, we continued on to Paris to yet another church to pick up a pastor and his family who would be coming to Marseille to help us in our church. Spending the night there before our long drive home the next day, we ventured out into the warm, summer evening in the City of Lights in search of something to eat. We were tired and it was already about 10 p.m., so we settled on a quick sandwich. We were discussing whether or not to go take in the splendor of the view of the Eiffel Tower at night, an absolute must on anyone's bucket list, which I had already experienced but my husband had not, when we received a phone call. Hannah had been trying to conceive for about 6 months and had been growing more and more concerned as to whether she could conceive at all. I don't recall the words she chose as she spoke that night, I only remember screaming with joy and announcing to all in the little restaurant that my daughter was going to have a baby! The small crowd there erupted with applause...a moment I will never forget.

No longer tired, but instead energized by the excitement of the news, we were now compelled to visit the Eiffel Tower in celebration. There, another moment took place that I will never forget. As if the Eiffel Tower at night isn't magical enough all by itself, we were standing directly under it, bubbling over with excitement for our daughter, and my husband took me in his arms and kissed me. It was as if all was right with the world, and the whole universe was in perfect harmony at that moment solely to accord me the purest, most complete joy I had ever felt. As long as I live, that will remain one of my top treasured experiences.

France, the Eiffel Tower, my husband and I in unity, and the news of a long awaited baby...life just doesn't get any better than that.

Months passed, and the joy was replaced by the reality of the distance between me and the beings I cherished... another one soon to be added. My husband had compassion and purchased a plane ticket for me to be in America for the birth of Hannah's first child, whom she learned was a boy.

It was a surreal moment when I saw Nile Alexander Hosni's face pushed out of my daughter and into the world. I was the first one to see him and greet him and at my shrieks of joy the nurses handed me the instrument to cut his umbilical cord...with their guidance of course. An immediate bond of unfathomable love was forged. No words could ever describe the experience of holding my child's child. When my first child, Austin, had his first baby, we had only been in France for a couple of months and I was not able to be there. That was an incredibly difficult time for me...my first grandchild, and I had always been there for all my children, every important event of their lives. I did not meet my first grandchild, Luke, until he was almost 1. It is very expensive to fly back and forth from France to the U.S. and so it was the same thing with my son's second child, Dylan. By the time Hannah was pregnant, Charlie's father had passed away and left him a bit of money, and so I was immensely thankful to be there for the birth of Nile, my third grandchild.

I was able to stay for six weeks and be of help to Hannah

and bond even deeper with Nile. Unfortunately, the day arrived when it was time for me to return to France. Etched in my mind forever is the somber drive to the airport. There had been too many teary goodbyes in our lives and so we made a pact to only say, "See you later", as if it would only be a day or two. Sort of a mind game, but uttering anything else would have caused our hearts to implode. I exited the car and peered into the back seat to have one last look at Nile; thank God he was asleep in his car seat, had he been awake I would not have been able to look into his eyes and walk away to board a plane that would distance me some 5,000 miles from him. I kissed his forehead...and with all my force tried to contain the flood of tears welling up inside me, but the dam broke and I sobbed, shook my head back and forth to my daughter signaling that it was too much to bear, turned and mournfully yet methodically made my way into the airport. I don't remember boarding, in fact, half the flight I was catatonically numb. This was the hardest thing I ever had to do...or so I thought. I did not know what laid ahead for me in just a couple of months after my return to France.

We were broadsided by another heartache. We were on our way home from church one evening when we received a phone call; in complete contrast to the joyful call we had received from Hannah announcing her pregnancy, this was the kind of call a parent does not want to receive. It was someone who worked for our church back home gravely telling us that we needed to call our pastor immediately. He would not give any details, he just said our pastor had been trying to reach us and we needed to call as soon as possible. Though no details or even the subject matter had been mentioned I instinctively knew it had to do with Sam and my heart pounded with fear all the torturous fifteen minutes of the drive home. Though we had received the call on our cell phone urging us to call our pastor, that was a brief few minutes so it was not too costly, however, a cell phone call from the U.S. to France or vice versa is extremely expensive and so we needed to make this call from our home phone. I raced ahead of my husband up the stairs and in a flash had the phone in my hand nervously dialing the number. Though my mind was comprehending the words being spoken on the other end of the line, my heart could not grasp or respond to the gut-wrenching news. Sam was out of his mind and in a dangerous physical state as well; he, already a thin person, had lost twenty pounds and was having to be force-fed. He was uttering unintelligible, diabolical rants, did not recognize his own sister, and was clearly taken over by some evil force. I knew that he had fallen in with a wrong crowd of friends he had made at the job he took after high school, I knew he had started smoking pot; I did not know at that point all he had dabbled in. To this day, I believe that one of those so-called friends was a Satanist. I tell Sam's story with his full permission.

I had just seen Sam on my visit to America for Nile's birth. In fact, he had moved in with a roommate who lived in the apartment just above Hannah's. He was working at a restaurant near the beach that had a hotel above it. He made friends with a guy a bit older than him whose job it was to sit in a small room watching the surveillance camera of the hotel, on the lookout for any crime or abnormal behavior. The guy actually lived in this small room. One night, wanting to go out for a while with his friend, he asked Sam to come and take his place for a few hours watching the surveillance camera. It was already late, about 10 or 11 at night, and Sam had just worked a full shift at the restaurant so he was exhausted. He watched for a while, switching back and forth between the surveillance and a DVD from the guys collection; it was some sort of homemade horror film…first mistake, and some odd occurrences started to happen. Sam accredited it to being overtired and thought he would close his eyes and rest a few minutes. Instead, he lay down on the guy's bed and fell into a deep sleep. He awoke to the guy and his friend standing over him laughing and asking him if he wanted some water. He was thirsty so he took the bottle offered to him…second mistake. Isn't it a bit odd to wake someone up and offer them water while laughing? Wake him and say that he was home and Sam was free to go now…yes, but to wake him up, laughing, offering a bottle of water in the middle of the night was suspicious, to say the least. Sam fell back asleep for a short while but soon started feeling strange. It was morning now and he had an early shift that day so even though his heart was racing he prepared for work.

He tried his best to shake off the bizarre thoughts and pounding heart and continue to work but to no avail. He began having a terrible stench fill his nostrils and then heard voices telling him that it was his own rotting flesh and that he was going to die. He was now panicking and told his boss he wasn't feeling well and needed to leave. His boss, having seen how strangely Sam had been acting and also his grim countenance agreed to let him go. I cannot tell you all that transpired after he left work, Sam does not remember and we only discovered a few clues in the aftermath the following day. I only know that in the evening he showed up at Hannah's door in a state I never wish to see anyone in again. His eyes were fully dilated, sweat jacket hood pulled over his head, panicked expression as cold, sweaty hands grabbed mine as he begged me to call my husband. He nervously wrung his hands on mine and pleaded, "Call dad, I need to talk to dad." I tried to calm him down and find out why he so desperately wanted to speak to his father, reasoning with him that because of the time difference, in France it was about 3 a.m. He tried to tell me what happened but started screaming with fear. We were all in the living room, including Nile who was only a few weeks old at the time. Hannah was freaked out and concerned for Nile as well so I took Sam into the bedroom. He would calm down for a few minutes and it was Sam looking into my eyes, but suddenly his eyes would dilate, he would let out a shriek, and then it was no longer Sam looking at me. It was as if he was taken over, which I tried to deny, but when I would try to calm him back down and say Sam, a voice, not Sam's, would angrily say…"Don't call me Sam." I was not capable of fully digesting what was happening, but through the intermittent presence of Sam and this other force, I was able to extract the story of the previous night's happenings, the bottle of water, and the morning at work with the voices. I concluded that the bottle of water had been drugged and did a quick search on the internet to determine the possible drug. I found one that mentioned racing heart, which he had, that was sometimes used as a date rape drug. As I read on I was convinced this was what had been given to him and because of the dangers associated with it, I whisked him off to the hospital. He grew calmer the closer we got to the hospital and by the time they hooked him up to a heart monitor his heart rate was normal. They did a few other tests and said he was fine. I told them of the suspected drugging but they told me they can only screen for major drugs like heroin, cocaine, and a few others and that with all the new drugs out there it would be impossible to detect...at least at their facility. We drove home to sleep. I slept on one couch and Sam slept on the other so I could keep an eye on him through the night. He awoke a couple of times, which I sensed, as only a mother can...I looked at him across the room, told him he was alright and to get some sleep, and he did. Morning came and he seemed to be fine, though a bit worn out and foggy headed from the ordeal. I was to return to France in just a few days and did not feel comfortable leaving him. I spoke to my pastor and explained everything as best I could. He offered to have Sam move into his home and assured me that he would be ok. Sam was all too happy to move in with the pastor; whatever went on in his apartment upstairs after coming home from work that day had frightened him to the point that he would not even enter that apartment again. We had to collect all of his belongings for him. I made sure Sam was well settled before I returned to France, both of us believing that horrible ordeal was behind us. Like waking from a nightmare, I shook it off and tried to forget.

It seemed that whatever happened to him was a one-time occurrence and all was well now...until the night of the phone call, when the nightmare worsened.

Having recounted these previous events, it is obvious why my gut told me it had to do with Sam before calling our pastor as we had been asked to do, and in spite of the fact that it had been at least two months since that first episode.

Our pastor, along with others from the church prayed and helped Sam as much as they could, hoping he would come out of it without them having to worry us since we were so far away. It came to a point though that all were concerned about his life. He refused to eat and had gotten so thin so they would have to force protein drinks down him to make sure he had some nourishment. He lost his faculties and had to wear an adult diaper, and a voice not his own was spewing ghoulish rants. Due to the severity now of his condition we were being not only informed but asked to make a decision. Our pastor told us that some were of the opinion that Sam should be put in a psychiatric hospital for surveillance and put on medicine, others said it was a spiritual matter and this evil force would be conquered and have to leave with continued prayer. We chose the latter and I am eternally thankful we did. I believe that if we had put him in a psychiatric hospital that he would still be there today doped on psych drugs and I would have lost my son. Instead, after about a week and much prayer, God won; good will always conquer evil. That was 8 years ago and today Sam is not only completely in his right mind and healthy, but he has been married for 4 years and is a chef at a high end restaurant. Was he drugged by the water? Was the friend a Satanist through whom an evil spirit entered Sam? We may never know…but it doesn't matter; what matters is that like the old adage says, "The proof is in the pudding." I know there might be skeptics and naysayers reading this that do not believe these spiritual forces exist, but had you seen Sam in that condition, you would believe.

My daughter Hannah, even though Nile was only 3 months old at the time, would go there daily and pray for her brother. He did not even recognize her. She called me one night crying, telling me that it was a good thing I was not there to see him like that because I would not have been able to handle it. I believe she is right, though it was extremely painful for me to know all this was going on and I was 5,000 miles away and could do nothing but pray. However, something miraculous happened in the heat of it.

It was a Sunday night and I was home alone. My husband and daughter Madelon had gone to church; I could not muster up the will and strength to go and try to hide my tears and fears behind a smile, but I couldn't bear to talk about it either, so I stayed. As soon as the door closed at their departure I threw myself on my bed and sobbed…then let out a guttural scream from the agony of my heart, "Jesus! I just want to hold my son until he is better! … I know that I can't, but you can so please hold him for me." It was not until much later when Sam was alright and we were able to speak about what happened that we pieced it all together. Without me saying anything at first, he began to tell me that he remembered very little of what went on during that time but that right before he came out of it, he saw a vision of me lying on my bed holding him! I had goose bumps everywhere and told him about the night I had been sobbing on my bed wanting to hold him and asking God to hold him for me. Then we both had goose bumps as we realized that it was that same night, at the exact moment of my prayer most likely, that Sam saw me on my bed holding him, and it was the following day that he was free of this evil spirit.

Again, I am not trying to preach to you or debate theologies, I am simply recounting the facts, sharing the stories of my pain and the higher power that I believe helped me through them.

Having gone through so many heart-wrenching incidents, I was completely spent. I was heartsick and my only cure was to return to my children. My deep love for the French people and their country was no longer enough to carry me through. I cried out to God to go home. I sensed that same inner voice, which I believe to be the voice of God, telling me that when it was time to go home, neither my husband or our pastor would be able to stop it...but by the same token, if it wasn't yet time to go home, there was nothing I could do about it. That voice reassured me that my life was in God's hands—not any human's hands, and when it was time, He would bring me home. I felt such a peace and was completely resolved that all was part of my destiny and that I would soon be home. I felt free to continue to care for the people of our church because I now felt cared for. One month later, we received an email from our pastor that it was time to come home…they had found a pastor to take over for us.

Surely I had heard from God that my life was in his hands; it was evident that He had orchestrated all this. Not only was my life not in my husband's hands or my pastor's hands, but I reflected on another time when it was revealed to me that my life hadn't even been in my parents' hands.

My birthdate is 5-8-58, and my mother always told me that I was born in room 558. She never forgot because she was struck by the oddity of all the 5's and 8's surrounding my birth. Not only did I grow up with the knowledge of this, but 5's and 8's seemed to follow me throughout my life. Forever showing up in addresses where I lived and other countless ways. Even my brief period in the Brownies as a child, my troop number was 888. I never thought too much about it but it occurred often enough to take notice.

One incident I will never forget was on one of my visits to America. I was driving my daughter's car alone going to get food for us all and was listening to whatever CD she had in. It was one of those players that you can put several disks in at a time. A song suddenly came on whose words were describing exactly what I was going through and I started to cry. A floodgate was opened as I felt a cleansing release of all I had held inside and I had to pull the car over, not being able to see through the tears. I loved the song and wanted to find out the title of the CD and the song so I glanced at the screen and saw that it was CD number 5, song number 8. I sobbed even harder now; those numbers had always been associated with my life and I felt like this time it was a message that God was with me and for me.

One day, we had a visiting pastor stay with us in France and he started talking about some recent discovery having to do with numbers. I had always shied away from digging into the meanings of numbers; being a Christian I did not want to live my life by numerology. However, this pastor reminded me that there was always significance to numbers in the Bible; God is a god of order and certain numbers held spiritual meanings. 1 is the number of unity, 3 is the trinity, 7...like 7 days in the week, is the number of completion and perfection. I decided to do a biblical search on the numbers 5 and 8. I learned that 5 is the number of grace, and 8 is the number for new beginnings—also the number for Jesus—in Greek, the number value given to the letters of his name add up to 888. At this discovery, a healing flood rushed through my veins. Grace and new beginnings—my mother had tried to cause a miscarriage by belly flops in a pool, my life had been spared from a drug overdose, suicide attempt, gun in my face by a thief in the store and countless car accidents. How many times God had shown grace and given me a new beginning. I may have been an unplanned accident to my parents, but I was in no way an accident to God. My life had always been and forever would be in his hands alone.

The pastor who was to take our place had to obtain his visa and finalize some other paperwork before coming. It was the end of summer, and knowing that we would soon return, we sent Madelon ahead of us to give her the time to get settled before school in September. She stayed with a family until we could join her. Due to these two situations, Charlie and I had a period of time alone. This had never been the case; when we married I already had Austin and so we were instant parents, and Hannah came along a year afterward. It was an important time in our marriage and we gained a deeper understanding of each other. By November, it appeared that it would only be a few more weeks until the new pastor would arrive. Charlie had some unfinished business in preparing for the switch-over but knew I was anxious to return with all the holidays coming up, and so he sent me ahead of him, expecting to join me in a few weeks.

I made it home in time to celebrate Thanksgiving with my children and my heart was full and whole. As Christmas approached, I planned and bought all the delicious foods I had longed to prepare for them but couldn't while separated in France. Reminiscing while decorating, shopping, laughing and baking, it was a dream come true; a stark contrast to that lonely Christmas spent with just Madelon and me and my husband who was ill.

It was not so cheery for my husband though, who was alone in France. I missed him but knew he would join me shortly…or so I thought.

There were complications with the pastor obtaining his visa to enter France; what was once believed to be a few weeks apart turned into an indefinite, unknown number.

Unbelievably, we spent a total of 5 months apart. It was April, just before Charlie's birthday, when he was finally able to join me.

Those 5 months apart were brutal but revelational. Missing Charlie terribly caused me to reflect quite a bit on our relationship and the ups and downs of it. I realized that one of the things that angered and drove me crazy about him was also, in fact, one of the things I loved best. He had a calm steadfastness about him that I sometimes mistook for aloofness. It was infuriating in the midst of a crisis to feel like he was completely unresponsive while I freaked out, fell apart, and desperately needed him to react! One day, fed up, I told him that I could come in and tell him that we just won a million dollars...or I could come in and tell him that one of the children just died and he would give the same non-response. With the calm of a heart surgeon he'd give a subtle nod of the head, and a practically whispered... uh-huh. Obviously, this was an exaggeration, but an illustration used to prove my point. Now, having to face situations and make daily decisions without him, I was aware of how much I needed his steadfast calm. I was the emotional one who overreacted and needed the balance he brought. What if we both freaked out emotionally? No, I needed him to keep me grounded, but I also realized during this time that he needed me as well. Calm is good, procrastination is not. I am the one that wants to pay the bill the second we get it, the one who is always punctual, etc. and he sometimes needed me to light a fire under him. We balanced and completed each other like 2 matching puzzle pieces. I was more thankful for him than ever and it was reciprocal. By the time he finally arrived in April, we were ecstatic to be reunited and more in love than we had ever been.

Returning to America was in one sense a relief, but it was also the end of a dream. Ever have a really good dream and then be so disappointed when you woke up to find it was just a dream? It felt a bit like that for me settling back into the routine of life in the United States—a rude awakening; the dream was over. Even though towards the end of our years in France the dream had turned into a bit of a nightmare due to all I suffered through with my children, I still loved the French people and their country and it will forever be an enchanted land of dreams for me. Who and what was I now? Where did I fit into the puzzle? A bit of an identity crisis brought back feelings of inadequacy and comparing myself to others. I did not want to go down that all too well-traveled road again. All this drudged up old wounds from my past, again. That is when I discovered the French Literature class I have been attending for six years, and where my soul is comforted every Tuesday basking in the beautiful French language. It is also where I met Michele and Meesha and so many other heroes. There is such diversity there—different countries and backgrounds, different ages, and different stories we bring as we migrate from our battle-worn paths to this common watering hole of the French language that has marked all of our lives in one way or another.

I kept busy and even went back to teaching at the church school...trying to find my place. My fulfillment came from spending time with my children and grandchildren, but life is expensive in Los Angeles and I was obligated to spend much of my time working. I spent as much time as I could though trying to make up for lost time with my loved ones. By now, my son Austin had 3 children and Hannah had two. When Nile was 3, Hannah gave birth to Lilah...my little soul mate. She loves everything I do and we have become joined at the hip. On days when I am down, it is the image of her face that makes me want to get out of bed and live another day.

My most pleasurable memories all involve my children. I have never laughed as hard or as long as I have with my children— and I have never wept so sorrowfully as I have over my children. There was one more sorrow to come...with my last child Madelon. I had suffered through the teenage rebellion and harmful choices of Austin and Hannah, the trauma with Sam—Madelon had watched the folly of her siblings and also was witness to my heart being shattered by them. I somehow expected her to be wiser for it. She was my constant companion and supporter, and also the one who was most tapped into God. I suppose that is why it came as such a shock when she chose to go against all that she knew to be right; it was so unexpected. Even though I had experienced much with the other three, it was just so radical and opposite of her timid character that I think it broke my heart even more than the others.

She moved out of our home for a time; her choices were just in such opposition to our beliefs that it caused too much conflict. She had been my last child still at home so when she left, and under the circumstances she left, it brought a crushing, echoing emptiness too much to bear. I could not pass by her deserted, lifeless room without breaking down and blubbering. Where did I fail her, and would I really be able to endure yet another blow regarding my children? It didn't seem possible for my already worn heart...but I carried on with my daily functions, though heavily weighted down—what other option did I have? I was depressed on and off and on autopilot for 2 years. Just when I felt I could not go on another day, Madelon came to her senses about where the direction of her life was going, did an about-face, and moved back home. It has not been a painless, seamless transition, but she has constantly moved forward in the right direction. She is the most private of all my children and so I cannot disclose any details about her ordeal. It suffices to say that I lost her for a while, and I am eternally grateful to have her back.

My children are my greatest source of joy, but they are also my greatest source of pain, due to the traumas they have suffered, which most I have only alluded to. Some terrible things have happened to them at the hand of others, some pain was self- inflicted by their own poor choices. Yet, as always with me, God rescued them.

Now, all I want to do is protect my grandchildren from any harm or pain. Though I pray for them, I have learned one thing—actually it is something I read in a book once, but did not fully understand until I had to live it out. It was a story about a man who had been observing a butterfly trying to burst out of its cocoon. It seemed to be struggling so severely that he had compassion and decided to help. He took a pair of scissors and slit the cocoon open to free the butterfly. To his horror, it did not fly away, but tumbled out with crumpled wings. Puzzled, he searched for an answer and discovered that it is in the struggle to emerge that fluid is pushed from its swollen body out into the wings to cause them to expand. Without the struggle, it would never be able to fly. I was touched by the story when I read it, but over the years, blinded by my intense love for my children I did not recognize at times when I was either trying to keep them in their cocoon...or slit it open for them. We all have to struggle to find our own path. Nevertheless, it is our job as parents to protect our children from the wiles of the world—we must find a balance.

Like all of us, each one of my children still has struggles to face in life. I love them, pray for them, and guide them as much as they allow me to. I try mostly to lead by example. They all love me, and they all love each other, and this is a great comfort. All that we have been through, instead of tearing us apart, has created such a tightly knit bond between us that nothing could ever break it.

There are so many details left out, and multiple other stories of sorrow and laughter I could tell you about my life, but that would be superfluous for the theme and purpose of this book. I do, however, have one last story to tell you— one of forgiveness and healing and coming full circle.

Beyond the Pain

PISMO. THAT ONE WORD, previously just the name of a city to me, will forever carry a meaning deeper than I could ever explain, though I will try in the following lines. Pismo Beach is the last place my father lived before falling ill and moving to Iowa to live with my sister. He actually lived just a few minutes above it in the tiny town of Arroyo Grande, but the whole area is known as Pismo Beach...simply Pismo, to all who know it well.

Anyway, this is where my father wanted his ashes spread, along the beach of Pismo. Though my father died in June, my two sisters and I, because of our different schedules or distance, could not all join together for this event until September. My brother, though invited, did not attend. That is a whole other story of pain, which I will not delve into.

During the couple of months prior to our fixed date in September, I prayed much. The three of us sisters were all in such different places emotionally and spiritually. I had forgiven my father long ago, or so I thought. My sister Dori still had a lot of anger and hurt. My sister Kristin, like me, had forgiven, however; she was my father's caretaker in the end and she had become embittered all over again due to his belligerent, vile demeanor during his illness and final days. I was not sure how it would all play out because of our differences. I had found peace in regards to my father and did not want to be dragged down again into bitterness, even by my sisters that I love dearly. I understood and could validate their emotions, but I simply could not risk entering into the negativity surrounding my father that had so damaged my life already. I wanted to let it all go and remember something good about my father. That was the difference in our emotions; as far as spirituality, my sister Kristin and I are Christians; my sister Dori has a different set of beliefs, leaning toward Buddhism. Though there is some common ground in the belief systems, such as being kind and loving to others, there are some major differences as well. One of them being who Jesus is: just another prophet and teacher...or the son of God? Also, there is a different definition of Heaven.

Part of the completion of my peace in regards to my father came when I last visited him and had the opportunity to pray with him. In spite of everything in our past, I had compassion for him and wanted the assurance of him making it to Heaven. As we stood in front of his driveway, just before I got in my car to leave, I summarized what I knew from the Bible regarding faith, forgiveness, and the way to Heaven. It was not completely foreign to him since he and his family had gone to church when he was young. I told him that I wanted to be sure that I would see him in Heaven, then asked if he would like to pray with me. He responded quickly and said yes. I left there sobbing with a relief, a peace, and an assurance that I would indeed see my father again on celestial shores. A joyful closing of a chapter for me...it was the last time I ever saw my father. For this reason, I did not want that memory tainted by anything, and so I prayed earnestly leading up to our September Pismo date.

The day finally came and Krissy flew in from Iowa. Having followed all the rules and regulations of transporting the ashes of human remains, she arrived carrying a small black duffle bag containing the properly packaged ashes. I was waiting for her, with palpitating heart, by the baggage claim area. As soon as we spotted each other we ran and fell into a tearful embrace that transmitted perfectly and wordlessly the fusion of joy and sorrow that accompanied this trip. The joy of sisters reuniting after too long a time; the sorrow of burying a father with whom we had a very broken relationship, but now having to bear the weight and finality of the fact that there was now no hope of repairing it; he was gone forever. Our tears spent, for the moment, we shakily let go of one another, and as I did so I spotted for the first time the small black duffle bag. I broke down into tears again at the realization that my father was inside.

My sister is great at bringing comedy into grave circumstances; seeing my distress, she said to me, "Say hi to

Dad..then quickly said to him...come on, Dad, time to go." We both had a good chuckle, and moved forward.

Dori had already driven down from San Jose to L.A. for some business so we all met on a Friday morning and drove up the coast the three hours to Pismo. We were all excited; we had not all three been together for fifteen years! I had seen Dori, I had seen Krissy, but not at the same time. They had seen each other, but not with me there. With Krissy in Iowa, Dori in San Jose, and though I was now living in L.A., I had lived in France for eight years, so it is not so shocking that we had not been able to all be reunited before now. From the second we all entered the car, we smiled from ear to ear, talked and laughed the entire road trip. Every moment of our weekend was miraculous in one way or another.

Any trepidation about possible conflict soon dissolved into a unity I have never experienced prior to or since. It is as if we were one in every movement, emotion felt or decision made throughout the weekend. We were in sync, and every moment was perfectly orchestrated despite our differences. It was truly a supernatural experience; someone or something else was in control.

The last stop on the road to Pismo was the Dutch tourist town of Solvang. A place we had visited as children with my father's parents, and also a few visits separately as adults. It had been quite some time and we thought it would be fun to visit briefly and stop at a bakery Dori had told us about. Now, almost at our destination, we had no specific plans for the weekend's events except two. We were going to spread my father's ashes, and we were going to take our father to dinner, or rather, he was going to take us. There was a small amount of money left over that was not eaten up by his care in the facility, and it was going to pay for our weekend. Thank God for my sister Kristin, the constant comedian, who brought levity to every situation. She is the one that decided even before coming that since my father never did so while alive, he was going to take his 3 daughters to dinner.

We got our baked goods (*wink to my sisters) and strolled through the town taking turns carrying my father in his temporary home...the black bag. We browsed in a jewelry store and then moved on to a little clothing store right next to it. As we entered, Krissy instantly spied a dress that caught her eye and gasped, as did Dori and I, because we all 3 in unison realized that it came in 3 colors. One for each of us. The same idea flowed at the same moment in all of our minds—wear matching dresses to our dinner with Dad. Keeping with the lightheartedness and comedy we had been employing in order to help us cope, we started talking, of course, Krissy first, as if it were my dad speaking. "What! Oh, Dad...you want to buy us all matching dresses? How you spoil us!" Gaining momentum with the humor, as we started to look at some more private items of women's apparel and make some jokes, Krissy paused and said, "Dad, cover your ears...they're in there right?"

I'm sure some of you reading about our antics will think that we were being terribly disrespectful, but I am convinced my father would have approved. He cracked plenty of bad humor jokes himself in his day, probably also as a way to cope.

We were excited now, snapped a few pictures of us with Dad in the bag in Solvang, then returned to the car to continue on to Pismo. Before going to the hotel we decided to visit the home my father lived in before moving to Iowa, which now had been sold. Our road trip of laughter came to a grinding halt. The closer we got to his street, the more somber the atmosphere in the car grew. At last, we were in front of his driveway, and we stopped...and stared...frozen in time, as if in another dimension. I don't think any of us had anticipated feeling this way. Paralyzed for a few minutes, Krissy was the first to break the silence by saying in an almost panicked voice, "I have to get out." She bolted out of the car and stood motionless for a few moments in front of his driveway. Then, my sister, the comedic one, now bawled like a baby in front of the last house my father had lived in, which she had not seen in years. She had the overwhelming feeling that he was about to come down the porch stairs to greet her...as he had done so many times before. Seeing her in this state Dori and I got out of the car as well and tried to comfort her. I was also overcome by tears and we let them flow freely as we held onto each other. Finally catching our breath, Krissy decided to place the black bag in front of the house for one last picture there...for closure.

We drove on towards the hotel and wound up on a barren dirt road where Krissy and Dori started discussing maybe burying his ashes right then and there on the road since it was near his home. They thought it might be appropriate. We weren't sure we were ready to let go yet though. We had previously discussed doing it the following day at sunset, at the beach. I blurted out suddenly, intending to be serious, "No! We have to take him to dinner first!" I did not realize how hilarious that would be coming out of my mouth and we all burst into uncontrollable laughter. We were all in agreement that when the time was right we would know it and continued on with our plan to go to dinner with our father.

We got all dolled up in our matching, though each a different color, dresses and marched confidently into the restaurant as we were seated. However, we glanced up from the menu at each other and mocked ourselves as we each had pulled out a pair of glasses in order to read the menu. We giggled and declared that we were not such a bad looking group of old broads. We asked the waitress to take our picture to mark the event, dad in his bag on the table, and she captured a perfect photo! Of course, we were trying to be discreet and she had no idea what was in the bag. We jokingly asked her if she could just follow us around for the weekend taking pictures, to which she replied "Sure! I could even fit in a bag like that!" as she pointed to the little black duffle bag. Our eyes instantly widened with horror as we gulped—before we could say a word she had already turned and gone. She had no idea what she was inferring and as the alarm of her declaration calmed down, we soon found the humor in it…of course, and it kept us laughing through the weekend.

That night after dinner, we returned to the hotel

exhausted—emotionally spent, but fell asleep with a smile, content with the plans we had for the following day to walk down to the beach just before sunset and place our father in his final resting place.

The next morning as we were preparing for the day, Dori stepped outside to make a phone call and visit the pool area. She had forgotten to take her key, and Krissy and I, busy in the bathroom, did not hear her knock. She was outside for some time without us hearing, and as she leaned against the post just outside the room, she glanced up and was suddenly struck by the number of the room posted on the door in bold black paint. It was room number 611. To most, that means nothing. Even to us, under different circumstances, it might have meant nothing. But we were here for my father who had worked his whole life for the phone company, and 611 was the number for repair. We finally heard her knocks and opened the door, but instead of coming in, she motioned for us to come out and look at the number on the door. Surely we were aware of what room number we were in when we checked in, but with the emotion of the day and the long drive had not given much thought to it. Now, however, it seemed as if my father was sending us a message. We stepped back into the room to discuss it when all at once it hit me, and I screamed as an electric shock of goose bumps traveled from my feet all the way up to the top of my head as I spoke the words that I believed was the message, "Dad wants to repair the lines of communication between us!" Now my sisters instantly felt the same shock of goose bumps throughout their body...

all 3 of us were screaming feeling like electric sparks were flying off the top of our heads. I have no explanation for what happened, but I know that it happened. We are not crazy, and we all 3 experienced the same thing. Whether it was my dad, or God, somebody was sending us messages all weekend. I am recounting only the main events and not the entirety of all the minor details that would only mean something to us, but truly there was something being repaired... something being communicated, and we felt closer to my father now in his death than we ever did while he was alive.

We had plenty of time before sunset and wanted to go into town to shop, eat lunch, and just enjoy the sunny day in Pismo before carrying out the grave task we had come here for. Ever since our arrival in Pismo we had been seeing dragonflies everywhere. By the pool, which is a normal occurrence, but also on the freeway in front of the windshield, by the beach, and now it seemed every shop we went into had dragonflies on their merchandise! It is not odd to see dragonflies on occasion in the usual places one would find them, but the frequency with which we were seeing them, and the unusual places we were seeing them aroused a curiosity. Have you ever seen a pair of sunglasses with little metal dragonflies on the side? Krissy was looking for new sunglasses and picked up such a pair, unknowingly at first, until we noticed them there. After so many sightings, I sensed another message and pulled out my phone to do a Google search on the symbolism of dragonflies. Here is what I found: the dragonfly symbolizes change, transformation, as in self-realization, and emotional maturity and deeper understanding of life. The way the dragonfly scurries in flight across the water represents going beyond the surface, and looking deeper into the implications and aspects of life. Again, goose bumps, though not as electric. We were certainly starting to look deeper into things, but I sensed there was much more to come. I was compelled to purchase a pair of abalone dragonfly earrings that had caught my eye in the very shop where I pulled out my phone and made the discovery of their meaning.

We had gotten so attached to taking our black bag with us everywhere, feeling closer to our father with each minute of the weekend that passed. In our minds and hearts, we had shared jokes and laughter with him, dinner, tears, messages...we had bonded. As the time grew near to let go of him, we each began to dread it. Dori started a discussion about whether we should each keep a bit of his ashes and only spread the majority of them here. A thought none of us had entertained before, least of all Dori, who previously seemed to be the most bitter and detached, coming only to perform a duty, have closure, and spend time with her sisters. So much had been done in our hearts already. In the same manner as the rest of the weekend had gone thus far, we were all in unison about keeping part of him with us and began searching for the appropriate container to keep the memorial of ashes in. We found perfect little wooden treasure boxes, one for each of us, and now feeling physically and emotionally prepared for the evening's ceremony, decided to go have lunch.

We had already decided earlier that we wanted to eat

at a place known for their wonderful clam chowder in a bread bowl, but as we approached it we saw a never-ending line formed around the side of the building just to get in. Famished and hot, we decided to look elsewhere. Just across the street was a place called Cool Cat and I piped up and said, "Hey, Dad was a cool cat, let's go check out the menu." He was a cool cat in his younger years because he loved Elvis, and even looked like him at one point. We strolled up to the entrance and grabbed a menu. Coincidence? They had on the menu an Elvis Tuna Melt and a Blue Hawaii salad…the title of an Elvis movie. We truly felt our father's presence was with us, enjoying the weekend making us smile.

Time was running out and we needed to get back to the hotel and prepare everything before dusk. Since it seemed that we had been so led in every detail the entire weekend, we decided to just gather what we needed and proceed with the spreading of his ashes with no prepared speech or planned order, but let ourselves continue to be led. The black bag had remained sealed until now. Krissy opened it to take out the death certificate to show to Dori and I who had not yet seen it, and reality set in. We had truly enjoyed ourselves strangely feeling like our father really had taken us to dinner and accompanied us throughout the weekend, but now the truth shattered the bubble of our fantasy by way of the death certificate, and the contents of the bag staring us in the face…it was time to let go. We mournfully gathered up our treasure chests and the small flour scoop we intended to use for the ashes, stuck them in the bag, and gloomily and methodically marched single file down the long wooden stairs that led to the beach.

We wandered out onto the sand making our way toward the shore, but it didn't take long to realize that without a boat it would not be possible to spread the ashes out far enough on the water so that they would not just be back up on the shore in a second, and that did not seem right. We glanced back at the way we had come, and seeing the rocky cliffs, made the unanimous decision to find a cave or some kind of hollow to bury them in instead. We scoped out a small indent of a cave not far from the stairs we had come down, but coming up upon it realized that is was a well-trafficked area and we would have no privacy. We walked back out toward the shore but this time headed around the curve of a small rock formed mountain right there on the sand. I was leading the pack now, which as the eldest suddenly seemed appropriate, and I was more determined than ever to find the perfect place. Just rounding the corner, with my sisters trailing a bit behind, I saw it. There it was...the most perfect cave—just the right size, and beautiful green and gold colored rocks at the entrance and on the inside walls. I excitedly called to my sisters that I had found it, and they hurried now to join me. They instantly agreed it was perfect. We only had to stoop a bit to enter and immediately started to clear any debris in the center of it, then feverishly dug a hole. We took our places seated around it and Krissy once again unzipped the bag.

First, we poured a small portion of the ashes into each of 3 small sachets to be placed in the 3 treasure chests for our individual memorials. Though no words were exchanged at this point, we all moved in unison as if following some unspoken instructions…it just flowed perfectly. We each took turns pouring a scoop full of the ashes into the hole, and at some point began talking about my father.

We each shared a good memory of our father, one the other two were not aware of. We were all amazed because we had only ever remembered the harshness and cold distance of our father. We completed the task of emptying the ashes and began filling the hole with sand to cover it back up . As our hands worked in unison forming the mound we were suddenly aware of the beauty of the moment and stopped to snap a picture. As we did, we noticed that my sister Kristin had my father's hands. This started a conversation about who had what from him and we concluded that Dori got his whistle—he always whistled through his teeth and Dori likewise, and I have his eyes. At that point, after discussing the honorable things he had done, and the observation of the favorable traits we had gleaned from him, a wonderful revelation came and the words tumbled out…we were works of Art! My father's name was Art. We were Art Sherman's daughters, and that was not such a bad thing after all. We talked about what he must have suffered as a child with his father and that how could he have been any different with the poor role model he had. We concluded that he had done the best he could— that he, in fact, must have loved us, but simply never knew how to express that in a proper manner. Dori spoke it first, then we all agreed to never speak ill of our father again.

We noticed a feather nearby in the cave and thought it would be a perfect crowning for our mound; our father was part Cherokee Indian. We placed it on top to mark the spot, knowing the tide would soon rise to wash it away, but also knowing it would forever be marked in our minds and in the photo we took of it. There was one last thing to do— the only thing I ever did have planned to do...months before coming. It was a song I had to sing. Someone had shared it with me one day when I was distraught the day after my father's passing. I was at school teaching math to my 4th graders, trying to hold back tears, but my sorrow was obvious. Though I had prayed with my father, I somehow needed an assurance that he was in Heaven now. The students knew my father had died, and one of the 4th graders named Natalie kept looking at me with compassionate eyes and asking if she could pull up a song on my phone from YouTube to share with me. I kept telling her not now, trying to stay focused on math, but she kept insisting that I needed to hear it. Finally, no longer able to resist her imploring eyes, I played the song. I blubbered, as every word seemed to speak to me, giving me my answer.

Now, here in the cave, I was driven to sing it for my father and my sisters as a final closure. My voice trembled and cracked with emotion but I steadfastly continued. The words echoing in the cave and in my heart...*All these pieces..* (or ashes*) broken and scattered, in mercy gathered, mended and whole...empty handed but not forsaken..I've been set free..* my father was now truly free of all pain..I choked up even more but resiliently forced myself to continue...*Amazing* *grace, how sweet the sound...that saved a wretch like me...I once was lost but now I'm found.........You place your treasures in jars of clay* (or treasure chests)...at that realization of how perfect it all fit together—buying the treasure chests without a thought of remembering the words to the song, my voice was completely suffocated in the uncontrollable sobs shaking my whole being. My sisters encouraged me that I could and should finish the song, so with everything in my being I summoned up the strength and concluded my eulogy to our father.

Sometimes we have painful choices; things are not always black and white. During the liberation of France, the mother of a friend of mine saw a very young German soldier who was dying in the street near her house. She wanted to help him but knew she would be shot if she was seen doing so, considered a traitor. In that moment, however, he was neither a German nor an enemy; to her mother's heart, he was simply just a boy, dying alone in the street.

I felt a parallel now. For my sisters and me, sitting together in that cave, as we poured out into this hole in the sand what remained of our father, we now had a choice before us to forgive, not an enemy, not the root of all our pain and struggles, just a boy, who died alone in his pain. How easy it is to forgive knowing this.

We all three found a deep emotional healing and walked out of that cave transformed. As we set my father free, not only by releasing his ashes, but by forgiving him, we also were set free. The incredible peace I felt let me know that I had found the final key, forgiveness, and as I walked out of that cave, the corridor disappeared, and I walked out of that final prison door to freedom.

None of us has ever been the same since our miraculous weekend in Pismo. We talk about it and refer to it all the time. We are truly changed people, free to live and love and hurt again, knowing that it is all part of life, and that is ok.

Throughout my life, though dark clouds have always tried to darken the sun of that vision of the cross, it is the sun that will always triumph. Of course, it is clear to me now why God would use the sun as a vision to speak to me. My name is Dawn, like the morning sun. I am a work of Art, not an accident. I was born on 5-8-58 in room 558, and it is not a coincidence that I am finishing the work of penning this book this year, as I turn 58.

For Mandie
(who passed away during the writing of this book)

There's no marker for my body
No tombstone with my name
There's nothing I leave behind
To ever show I came

Though there were days that dragged so long
The years went rushing by
I didn't use them wisely
I wasn't prepared to die

Let others heed this warning
Spend each minute as if it's your last
For once it's gone it's gone
And how they go spinning past

Live and love with every breath
So there are no regrets when you meet death
But first, be sure your soul's anchored to a heavenly home
    on high
For no one thinks, "Tomorrow, I may die"

One last event happened to bring me full circle. Not so many months after Pismo, David Bowie died. Of course, my first thought was of Leslie. No one else on the planet could be as grieved as I was at that moment; it was not just *his* death, but also the death of an era, and the death of my youth to me. I had to find her. I had reconnected with her only once, briefly, some 25 years prior. At that time she had just gotten married, and I was already pregnant with my fourth. Our lives were in different places, and also I moved shortly after that to Little Rock. I had no other news of her during those 25 years. I couldn't remember her married name and she did not use her maiden name on social media. Long story short, through many Google searches and sites I found a list of Leslie's her age in the general area and when I saw the last name of one it clicked and I was sure that was her married name. I excitedly and nervously typed that name into Facebook and suddenly my dear long lost friend's face appeared before me. So many emotions and memories flooded my mind and heart. I sent her a message and waited eagerly. A few days passed...no response. I had noticed on her page that there had not been a new post for almost a year. Dread struck. "We are getting older," I thought to myself. What if she had passed away? Or...what if she did not want to be reminded of the past and was choosing not to contact me? I hung on to hope but one week later, a bit heartbroken, I accepted it and moved on.

One evening, while I was on Facebook, she sent me a message! She was overjoyed that I had searched for her and contacted her! She had all the same emotions as I did hearing of Bowie's death, and she also immediately thought of me. Though she was living about an hour from me, we agreed that we needed to meet as soon as possible or it would never happen. Life gets too busy and the best intentions are forgotten. We set a time to meet the soonest Saturday coming up.

As I sat there in the restaurant waiting for my dear old cherished friend, so many mixed thoughts and emotions overtook me. I was beyond ecstatic to see her again, but thought, what if it was an awkward meeting because we had become too different over the years? What if after 5 minutes we have nothing left to say? It felt like an eternity until she arrived. My doubts and fears turned out to be completely unfounded. The moment our eyes fixed on each other we gasped and laughed. She walked towards me with her arms extended and as soon as we hugged it was like going home. We talked nonstop for 4 hours to fill each other in on our lives. We could barely take a bite of our food or bother to stop long enough to take a sip of water. Our bond, even after all these years apart, was so deep that I instantly felt like I did back in Jr. High and high school—talking, laughing, and crying with my best friend. Neither one of us wanted to leave, but there were family and work obligations now that called to us. We did not part ways, however, without setting another date to meet.

That time as well we talked for hours…never enough time to finish all that was in our hearts to say before it was time to go. We have met several times since then, as often as possible with the distance between and responsibilities we both have. Every time, we are like giddy Jr. Highers, and we have vowed to never lose touch again. We even have a goal to travel to France together…just as we dreamed of so many years ago in high school. We are both so thankful for our friendship, and for my part, it has brought me back full circle to the origins of who I am at my core. It is, in part, her support, encouragement, and belief in me that has enabled me to complete this book.

Pain has no prejudices, it is a fact of this world, but this world is temporary; we are just passing through. There is, however, a beauty in the pain : the sun never looked so radiantly beautiful as it does when it peeks its head out after a fierce storm, home never looked so welcoming as it does after a long and difficult journey, and joy never vibrated as deeply as it does after a long and painful experience. When we have suffered greatly, not only do we have compassion for others in their sufferings, but we also rejoice so easily at the little pleasures in life. A true, heartfelt joy, not only for our own pleasures, but an honest celebrating of the joyful moments of others, as if it were our own. This is an art that is learned, and pain and suffering are our only instructors. Every act of kindness or love by our hand that brings a smile to someone else, bounces back to warm our own heart. This is how we take the broken pieces of our life and use them to build a beautiful mosaic. Two key factors: forgiving those who hurt us, and helping others. Forgive, not because the person who hurt you deserves it, but because you do. When we hold on to bitterness and anger it only damages our own life. Besides, you do not know what story hides behind the lines of their life, what pain has caused them to behave the way they have. Forgiving is not excusing the pain they have inflicted on you; it is going beyond your pain, finding the story behind the story of their life in order to separate the person from the injustice. Most people who hurt others have themselves been hurt. Learning about their pain can set you free from your own. In some cases one can not know their story, for example, if you were raped by a stranger. However, simply acknowledging that there must have been a story, their own prison of pain, can still help you forgive and unlock you from yours.

For some, slaying the dragon of sorrow once is enough. For others, like me, it is a process. Life will always have its ups and downs, joy and pain; that's life. I sometimes still have a bit of a knee jerk reflex of momentary panic when troubles come, that feeling of the rug being pulled out from under me like my world is falling apart. The dragon tries to resurrect. However, I have been to his lair and cut off his head; it is only his writhing body trying to frighten and intimidate me. Every time I confront him anew, brandishing my sword, it is a reminder of his defeat and he loses a little more power over me.

At least I have discovered his lair; he dwells in the dark caves of memories of pain. Dealing with our past is like a child afraid of the dark and the monster under the bed; switch on the light and the monster disappears. Though we might have had some all too real and painful traumas in our life, it is the memories of pain and fear in our head that paralyze us, keeping us from healing and progressing in life. However, revisiting those events, forgiving, realizing that they no longer have power over you, is like turning on the light… the monster/dragon disappears. I urge you to visit the lair and turn on the light. Forgiving, and helping others, these are the things that have brought healing and wholeness to my own soul.

The most breathtakingly beautiful mosaics are not the ones fashioned from pre-cut, smooth, perfectly formed tiles, but instead are the ones formed from broken, jagged pieces of porcelain or sea glass, with distinct shapes and character. The larger pieces must be hammered into smaller ones; the rough ones must be sanded smooth. Then, the muddy grout that is smeared everywhere to fill in the cracks between the pieces to hold the design together must dry before it can be cleaned off. It is work, and it is messy, but the end result is well worth it.

You have read of Meesha, who did not slay the dragon, Michele and Sophie, who gloriously slew the dragon, my father, who spent his life pretending the dragon did not exist, and me, who has exposed to you the hidden lair of the dragon. There are so many other heroes. Some others in my class include a woman who lost her only son, a few others who lost their husband, another who lost both husband and son, some survivors of the war, others survivors of cancer or some other dreaded disease. There are stories from Russia, Germany, Iran, Italy, France as well as many states all over the U.S. There are many in our church as well: a husband whose wife died of a brain tumor leaving him with six children, single mothers working endlessly just to provide for the children they wish they could stay home and take care of, broken hearts, broken families, broken lives...the list goes on. Look around you, they surround us. Will you notice them and help them despite your own pain? Can we all help each other through life? Will you stay focused on your own dark sky...or look up at the stars shining all around you?

For me, it is God who placed the sword in my hand, giving me the ability and courage to venture into the lair and conquer the pain. It has been a long and difficult journey and battle, but I have tried along the path to offer to others the hope and healing I have received along the way.

Where Do You Turn?

Where do YOU go when pain abounds?
When comfort and answers are not to be found?
Some say God does not exist

They look up and angrily shake their fist
So they bear it alone...the atheist

Others believe there IS a Creator
Though they think of themselves as something greater
They call upon faith, call upon love
Yet, never lift their eyes above
They look inward for strength, to what they're made of

It takes a humble soul to call
Upon the maker of us all
To place our brokenness in His hand
And trust He has a greater plan
That He'll mend our life as only He can

Don't cry alone, don't shake your fist
Don't seek your own strength and help resist
There's a God who wants to heal our pain
And turn each loss into a gain
If only you would call on His name

Healing is a process; I continue to walk down its path. I have grown and healed so much already and I am certain of this: there IS hope and life and joy beyond the pain. I am finally at peace with who I am and who I am not.

Whether you had a spouse that died too young, suffered through the Holocaust, been sexually molested, had your heart broken by a father, mother, sister, brother, friend or lover, no matter what form your pain comes in, know that it will come. Like death, pain will come to us all. No one can choose not to experience pain; our only choice is what we will do with it. Will we overcome, slay the dragon and use our experiences to be the other strap and help carry the pain of others? Will we remain bottled up full of poison; or are we willing to be broken open and poured out like a balm for the healing of others and ourselves? I have chosen, in writing this book, to be broken open. What will you choose? Hopefully, you will find yourself and find your path to healing somewhere between the lines of this book. Then, with the help you find, help others to take the broken pieces of their life and build a beautiful mosaic to add to the beauty of this world. I promise that there IS a beauty to be found in the brokenness. Have hope; tomorrow is another day, and one never knows what that day may bring. Why some lives are so full of pain while others are scarcely grazed by it will always be a mystery; don't waste time wondering why, just use your pain as a tool. People who have suffered are deeper and more compassionate—count yourself as chosen and special.

With the pendulum now in a very balanced middle, I conclude with these two things: A David Bowie song "Fill your Heart" which can be found on YouTube, and which contains the line, "the dragons have been bled", the Beatles song "Blackbird"...take these broken wings and learn to fly, and these passages from the Bible...

Galatians 6:2 "Carry each other's burdens, in this way, you will fulfill the law of Christ."

Psalm 126:5-6

5 Those who sow with tears
will reap with songs of joy.
6 Those who go out weeping,
carrying seed to sow,
will return with songs of joy,
carrying sheaves with them.

I have written this book through tears, hoping to carry some sheaves with me into joy and healing. My life is now literally an open book…and that is both frightening and liberating all at the same time.

If truly the pen be mightier than the sword
Let my words pierce the heart to win souls for my Lord

If I should die tomorrow
Place no flowers by my grave
Shed no tears for the days I'll miss
For my soul the Lord shall save

My father in high school.

My on my eighteenth birthday at Leslie's house.

Me and my sisters after exiting the cave where we buried our father's ashes.